D0936506

KIPLING'S 'LAW'

KIPLING'S 'LAW'

A study of his philosophy of life

SHAMSUL ISLAM
Department of English, Panjab University, Lahore

With a Foreword by
J. M. S. TOMPKINS
formerly Reader in English, University of London

ST. MARTIN'S PRESS NEW YORK

Copyright © 1975 Shamsul Islam

All rights reserved. For information, write:
St. Martin's Press, Inc., 175 Fifth Avenue, New York, N.Y. 10010
Printed in Great Britain
Library of Congress Catalog Card Number: 75-24793
First published in the United States of America in 1975

823.
K57zshk

203714

To my Parents and Anne

11-20-80—Barnes & Noble $17.25

Contents

Acknowledgements

I owe a great debt to Dr J. M. S. Tompkins, the distinguished Kipling scholar, who read the typescript in one form or the other, made many invaluable suggestions, gave me an insight into Kipling's mind and art, and encouraged me greatly. In fact without her support, advice and affection, the book would never have seen the light of day. I am also beholden to her for writing the foreword for my book.

I wish to express my deep sense of gratitude to these members of the faculty at McGill University, Montreal, Canada: to Professor Alan Heuser for his advice, valuable criticism and patience, and to Professors Joyce Hemlow, Alec Lucas and Louis Dudek for their suggestions and encouragement.

I am grateful to Dalhousie University, Halifax, Canada for the award of a Killam Visiting Fellowship which made it possible for me to use the Stewart Kipling Collection at Dalhousie University in 1967–8.

I must also thank the British Council for the grant of a Research Bursary for summer 1974 which enabled me to meet a number of Kipling scholars and use the facilities at the British Museum.

Thanks are also due to Mr R. L. Green, editor, *The Kipling Journal,* for permission to reprint those portions of my book which first appeared there.

The publishers and I are grateful to Mrs Bambridge and Doubleday & Co. Inc., New York, for permission to quote the copyright material by Rudyard Kipling.

Finally, to my wife my thanks for her tactful remonstrances whenever I dropped the idea of completing this project.

S.I.

Foreword

Hostile critics of Kipling sometimes allude, as a dismissive gesture, to the 'Indian' view of his work. It is not a conclusive manoeuvre for, apart from the fact that Indian subjects occupied him for less than half his writing life, the Indian view of him varies widely. Nirad C. Chaudhuri read *The Jungle Book* with delight from childhood to maturity, but was for long unwilling to face the wounding slights he expected to find in the adult tales. When he did face them he certainly found matters of offence, but he also found *Kim,* which he proclaimed the finest story about India written in English. A student of mine was moved by what he considered the English undervaluing of Kipling's work to select it as the field of his Ph.D. thesis. He too, on more searching enquiry, found in it inaccuracies, misjudgements and evasions, but also concluded that no one, Indian or English, had described aspects of Indian life better than Kipling, or in a way more likely to rouse homesickness in an Indian overseas. Then there are the comparisons with E. M. Forster, or occasionally with Flora Annie Steel, falling now one way, now another, according to the criteria applied. Many of these differing voices are Bengali, and most of them are Hindu; but the voice that has not hitherto been heard is that from the Panjab, Kipling's home province, then, though not now, wholly a part of India, where he was posted for the first five years of his writing life.

In *Something of Myself* he recounts how he was sent down to work on the *Pioneer* at Allahabad, 'hundreds of miles to the southward', and how 'the North-West Provinces, as they were then, being largely Hindu, were strange "air and water" to me'. He adds in quiet explanation: 'My life had lain among

Muslims, and a man leans one way or other according to his first service.' This inclination is more warmly expressed in 'William the Conqueror', where the small party of civilians, returning from famine work in Madras, delight in the winter landscape of the Panjab, 'the layers of wood-smoke, the dusty gray blue of the tamarisks, the domes of ruined tombs, and all the smell of the white Northern plains', and hear with pleasure 'the large open names of the home towns . . . Umballa, Ludianah, Phillour, Jullundur'. During his early years in this Province he developed his sympathy with Islam, responding readily to the pride and independence of the Muslim, and to the discipline of a fighting faith and an exacting education. It can be found, twenty years later, revivified and flooding his mind with urgent memories and familiar responses, in his description of his first return to the East in *Egypt of the Magicians*. However penetrating his curiosity and compassion in Hindu lands, however memorable the figures that his blended humour and tenderness evoked there, these lands were never 'home' to him, as the Panjab was.

It is therefore a matter of interest that Dr Shamsul Islam, whose book breaks new ground in Kipling studies, is a Panjabi and a Muslim, living and working in Lahore, where Kipling spent the five years of his 'first service'. Here, in spite of violent changes, it is possible to follow his subject's steps and to see and hear much of what he saw and heard. Dr Islam tells me that he can sometimes detect the characteristic Panjabi word-play under the dialogue in the tales. But I should do him a disservice if I left it to be assumed that his main purpose is to mount a counter-offensive from the Panjabi angle. His book is a piece of strict scholarship, valid and illuminating in any context, an attempt to define, as far as is possible, Kipling's insistent and elusive concept of the Law. His sense of fellow-citizenship lies quietly behind his scholarly and logical approaches to this problem and provides the implied sympathy without which, though useful detached investigations can be made, there can be no just assessment of a writer since there is no sustained impulse to understand, in depth, what he said and why. Dr Islam is well aware that certain parts of Kipling's writings have given offence to Indian readers and, by reflection, to English ones, and he knows what the offence is; but such notorious tales as 'The Head of the District' and 'The Enlightenments of Paget M.P.' do not, in fact, offend him and he is able to read them without disturbance and to estimate how much of them is true and probable.

The complex of ideas conveyed by Kipling, all through his writing life, under the name of the Law has been frequently cited but not analysed with any strictness. It was seriously held and deeply felt. It was not confined to any particular body of enactments, but was a universal principle of order, at both social and individual levels, laying on men the obligations of disinterested suffering and positive action. Dr Islam pushes towards a closer definition of what Kipling, a creative artist and no logician, left loosely defined and, at times, apparently inconsistent. He traces the influences of his formative years under which this concept took shape, and considers the contributions to it of India and England, the elements it drew from the various faiths he encountered and from experiences so diverse as the 'sahib-consciousness' of his childhood and young manhood and the harsh lessons in obedience in his adoptive home at Southsea and at school. He links Kipling's need for such a Law to his temperament and outlook, his experiences of profound despondency and frustration, his sense of the hostility of the universe and the role of the 'Dark Powers' in life. Against the pull of a philosophic nihilism the Law is a weapon and a defence.

Dr Islam's main argument is supported by quotations from Kipling's verse and prose. There is much that is interesting and novel here, especially in his comments on the children's books, and doubtless some things that will be found controversial. He is a young scholar, aware of his age and the ages behind him, and he sees Kipling as a man of his time, open to its pressures. He does not condemn him for opinions which rose naturally in his environment, or slant his interpretations of the tales in accordance with the predilections of the mid-twentieth century. His book fills a gap in Kipling studies with honourable and intelligent work.

J. M. S. Tompkins

1 Sources and Approaches

A KIPLING CRITICISM: A BRIEF SURVEY

Although Kipling was the most popular writer of his time, his literary reputation has followed an uneven course. There was a variety of Kipling criticism right from the start, but it was after the South African War that Kipling suffered from a violence of attack which is unparalleled in English literary history. At the turn of the century his critics often admired him for his craftsmanship, but they judged him on moral grounds without caring to read between the lines, generally dismissing him as a jingo imperialist and a superficial writer. To the serious detriment of his reputation, this negative view of Kipling became widely accepted.

This early negative attitude toward Kipling is best typified by the frequently quoted essays of Francis Adams and R. W. Buchanan. In his *Essays in Modernity: Criticisms and Dialogues* (1899), Adams praises Kipling for his artistry, but at the same time calls attention to Kipling's 'smartness and superficiality, jingoism and aggressive cocksureness, rococo fictional types and overloaded pseudo-prose' — and then he goes on to dismiss Kipling as an 'ill-educated, promiscuously receptive, little-brained, second-rate journalist, with all his sickening egotism and vanities'.[1] In a similar fashion, Buchanan in his essays in *The Voice of 'The Hooligan': A Discussion of Kiplingism* (1900) disparages Kipling as follows:

> The most extraordinary feature at this moment is the exaltation to a position of almost unexampled popularity of a writer who in his single person adumbrates, I think, all that is most deplorable, all that is most retrograde and savage, in the restless and uninstructed Hooliganism of the time.[2]

It was because of these and similar critical pronounce-
ments, which were generally accepted, that after his death in
1936 very little was written about him. In 1941 T. S. Eliot
took a bold step by publishing *A Choice of Kipling's Verse*,
with an introduction which ranged perceptively over both
verse and prose. In this essay Eliot defended Kipling against
the charges of racialism and jingo imperialism, pleading for a
dispassionate reassessment of him. Eliot's plea, however,
aroused a reaction among reviewers which amounted to con-
sternation.[3]

The same year also saw the publication of Edmund
Wilson's article, 'The Kipling That Nobody Read', in *The
Atlantic Monthly:* although in balance not a sympathetic
study, this essay directed attention to the remarkable development of Kipling's art in the later stories. Eliot's plea for
a reconsideration of Kipling coupled with Edmund Wilson's
essay led to a revival of interest in Kipling as a prose artist.
Hilton Brown's 1945 biography of Kipling, *Rudyard Kipling:
A New Appreciation,* was, as the title suggests, another
attempt to revive interest, but perhaps an unconvincing one.

The next decade brought signs of a change. In 1951
Bonamy Dobrée wrote a pamphlet in which he analysed
Kipling's thought, concluding that while Kipling was not a
first-rate writer, he was 'a very great craftsman indeed'.[4] In
1955 C. E. Carrington published his official biography of
Kipling: for the first time substantial information concerning
Kipling's private life was made available. The efforts at a
rehabilitation of Kipling as a consummate artist culminated
in 1959 with the publication of Dr J. M. S. Tompkins's book,
The Art of Rudyard Kipling, which remains the most perceptive scholarly study of Kipling's fiction to date.

With Dr Tompkins's study, Kipling's reputation as a first-
rate literary artist may be said to have been firmly established. However Kipling continues to be attacked for
immaturity of ideas, though in the recent past several able
defences of Kipling's thought and vision have been made.
Bonamy Dobrée started the fight as early as 1927 with an
essay 'Rudyard Kipling', in *Criterion,* 6 (Dec 1927)
499–515, later reprinted in *The Lamp and the Lute: Studies
in Six Modern Authors* (1929). In this article Dobrée ana-

lysed Kipling's philosophy of action in an objective manner and he called attention to the fact that Kipling's concept of the Empire has a moral side to it. Dobrée again wrote on Kipling in 1951 in the series 'Writers and their Work', and in 1967 he brought out a full length study of him, *Rudyard Kipling: Realist and Fabulist,* which however did not add much to what he had previously said on Kipling's philosophy of life.

Professor Dobrée's radical reappraisal was soon followed by several serious, scholarly studies of Kipling's thought. The most important of these studies are: Lionel Stevenson, 'The Ideas in Kipling's Poetry', *University of Toronto Quarterly,* 1 (July 1932) 467–89; Noel Annan, 'Kipling's Place in the History of Ideas', *Victorian Studies,* 3 (June 1960) 323–48; Richard Faber, *The Vision and the Need: Late Victorian Imperialist Aims* (London, 1966), with a chapter on Kipling; and Alan Sandison, 'Rudyard Kipling: The Imperial Simulacrum', in *The Wheel of Empire* (New York, 1967) — Sandison's study had of course appeared earlier in a slightly different form in 'Kipling: the Artist and the Empire', *Kipling's Mind and Art* (London, 1964), edited by Andrew Rutherford.

All of these studies, not necessarily entirely favourable to Kipling, endeavour to examine Kipling's thought, particularly his imperial theme, in an objective manner. They emphasise that Kipling's philosophy of life and its relation to the Imperial Idea is much more complex than has been realised, and that a concept of 'Law', which is central to Kipling's works, is not an ordinary idea. This is a welcome change in Kipling criticism, and the essays collected in *Kipling's Mind and Art* (1964), edited by Andrew Rutherford, as well as *Kipling and the Critics* (1965), edited by Elliot L. Gilbert, give a fair impression of this gradual shift in Kipling's position in the literary world since his death.

It may however be interesting to note that the Indians who have written on Kipling have invariably accused him of the oft-repeated charges of chauvinism, racialism and jingo imperialism. A. R. Sarath Roy, in an article for the *North American Review* 'Rudyard Kipling Through Hindu Eyes', considers Kipling to be a British propagandist engaged in

slighting the Indian character, with no understanding of
India.[5] In a brief essay in *Lippincott's Magazine* by 'An
Indian Student', the writer denigrates Kipling for his lack of
insight into Indian life.[6] Bhupal Singh, in *A Survey of Anglo-
Indian Fiction,* has come to the same conclusion.[7] Nirad C.
Chaudhiri is, however, to some extent an exception. In his
article, 'The Finest Story About India — in English', *Encounter,* 7 (Apr 1957) 47–53, Chaudhuri makes a perceptive
study of *Kim,* and he credits Kipling with having written
about India with insight and understanding. More recently,
K. Bhaskara Rao has published an interesting study, *Rudyard
Kipling's India* (Oklahoma, 1967), in which he claims to have
examined Kipling without getting emotionally involved with
the subject; but I am not sure whether Mr Rao has succeeded
in translating his purpose into reality, for he ends up repeat-
ing the old charge that Kipling's vision of India was a boy's
vision.

Thus we see that after a long period of eclipse, Rudyard
Kipling has certainly come into his own. He has been rehabili-
tated as a first-rate artist, but criticism has yet to come to
terms with his philosophy which, as we shall see, is one
closely tied up with politics, history and sociology.

B APPROACH USED IN THIS STUDY

The foregoing brief survey of Kipling criticism indicates that
the controversy about Kipling's ideas is hardly over and that
a study of his philosophy of life remains an open field. In
other words, 'the riddle of Kipling', to use Noel Annan's
phrase, is yet to be solved. Kipling scholarship in the past
decade, as it has been suggested in the last section, has done
the spade work in this regard — it has established a few
guidelines that an investigator should follow in his inquiry
about Kipling's thought. These guidelines may be summarised
as follows:

1. Kipling is a writer of depth and vision.
2. Kipling's imperial theme cannot be equated with British
   Imperialism, since the relation of Kipling's philosophy to
   the Imperial Idea is much more profound than has been
   suggested.

3. An investigation of Kipling's ideas must be based on a close study of his works in their totality, and not on a few isolated pieces used as crutches for projecting one's preconceived notions about him.
4. Kipling must be studied in relation to his age.

This study is in keeping with the modern trend in Kipling scholarship. It aims at an investigation of Kipling's philosophy, which he terms 'Law', on the lines indicated above. 'Law', a word which runs like a leitmotiv in his works, is not limited by the legal connotations of the word 'law', but is a much wider and rather fluid concept, denoting the code of life projected by Kipling in his writings. Kipling's vision of the universe, as will be made clear in the course of this study, is rather bleak. At every nook and corner he confronts the nameless, shapeless Powers of Darkness, Disorder and Chaos. However instead of submitting himself to the sway of these negative forces or falling into the escapism of the debauched Simla society or that of the opium dens of the slums of Lahore, Kipling opposes the Dark Forces heroically with what he terms 'Law'.

Nevertheless Kipling never defines what exactly he means by Law. Perhaps a precise statement of such a wide concept is impossible, and besides, one must keep in mind that Kipling is not a philosopher in the strict sense of the term. This lack of a definition of Law is mainly responsible for the general misinterpretation of Kipling, for a superficial reader, as most critics of Kipling are, can easily identify Kipling's Law with the Queen's Law, providing himself with another proof of Kipling's racism as well as of his die-hard, jingo imperialism. A careful perusal of Kipling's works will, however, show that his master-thought, vaguely defined though it may be, is very different. The following selection of references to the word Law from his works will demonstrate this difference, and at the same time, these quotations will underline the difficult problem of adducing an accurate interpretation of the nature of Kipling's Law.

In 'A Song of the English' (1893) England advises her children — the member nations of the Empire — in these words:

Keep ye the Law — be swift in all obedience —
Clear the land of evil, drive the road and bridge the ford.
Make ye sure to each his own
That he reap where he hath sown;
By the peace among Our peoples let men know we serve
the Lord![8]

The members of the Empire pledge their loyalty to Mother England and England answers:

I shall know that your good is mine: ye shall feel that
my strength is yours:
In the day of Armageddon, at the last great fight of all,
That Our House stand together and the pillars do
not fall. . . .
And *the Law* that ye make shall be law after the rule
of your lands. . . .
The Law that ye make shall be law and I do not press
my will,
Because ye are Sons of The Blood and call me Mother still.
(*DE* 178. Italics mine.)

The diversity in the nature of the Law is evident in these two quotations. In the first passage England explicitly enjoins upon her Sons the duty of keeping the Law, which she defines as eradication of evil, public works, peace, justice, and so forth; but in the latter passage she is flexible enough to allow her Sons to modify certain types of specific Law in accordance with their own traditions and local customs.

The ambiguity of the word Law becomes apparent in *The Jungle Books* (1894-95), in particular where we are told that there is a Law of the Jungle which is, however, not the one that we generally associate with the term 'Law of the Jungle'. Akela, the wolf, cries from his rock: 'Ye know *the Law* — ye know *the Law*. Look well, O Wolves!'[9] Later on Bagheera throws some light on the Law of the Jungle — he tells Mowgli:

All the Jungle is thine and thou canst kill everything that thou art strong enough to kill; but for the sake of the bull that bought thee thou must never kill or eat any cattle, young or old. That is *the Law* of the Jungle.
(7 16. Italics mine.)

Further on in *The Jungle Books* we learn that the Law does
not extend to all animals of the jungle, for Baloo, the old
teacher of the Law, advises Mowgli as follows:

> 'Listen, Man-cub,' said the Bear, and his voice rumbled like
> thunder on a hot night. 'I have taught thee all *the Law* of
> the Jungle for all the peoples of the Jungle — except the
> Monkey-Folk who live in the trees. They have no *Law*. They
> are outcasts.'
>
> (7 41. Italics mine.)

These words of Baloo recall the well known controversial line
from 'Recessional' (1897): 'Or lesser breeds without *the Law*
—'. (*DE* 329. Italics mine.)

In 'Dray Wara Yow Dcc' (1888) the fierce Pathan has his
own notion of the Law; thus he sneers at the English narrator: 'Your *Law!* What is your *Law* to me?' (4 9. Italics mine.)

In 'The Miracle of Purun Bhagat' (1894) Sir Purun Dass,
once a Prime Minister of an Indian princely state and now a
sanyasi (mystic, holy man) going about with a begging bowl,
passes through a busy Simla street on his way to his hermitage. He is stopped by a policeman who reprimands him for
obstructing the traffic, and 'Purun Bhagat salaamed rever-
ently to *the Law*, because he knew the value of it, and was
seeking for a *Law* of his own'. (8 181. Italics mine.)

Similarly the Lama in *Kim* (1901) is a follower of the Law
as he himself affirms: 'I follow *the Law* — the Most Excellent
Law.' (19 53. Italics mine.)

One recurrent note in Kipling's writings is that the Law
must be obeyed. This message is thus summed up in
'McAndrew's Hymn' (1893) as he addresses his engines:
'Now, a' together, hear them lift their lesson — theirs an'
mine:/ "Law, Orrder, Duty an' Restraint, Obedience, Discipline!" ' (*DE* 126) Similarly in the poem 'The Law of the
Jungle' which follows the story 'How Fear Came' (1894) we
are told:

> *Now these are the Laws of the Jungle, and many and*
> *mighty are they;*
> *But the head and the hoof of the Law and the haunch*
> *and the hump is — Obey!*
>
> (*DE* 560)

Nevertheless there are circumstances under which the Law ought not to be invoked, when the breach of it represents a more profound justice. This is illustrated by the poem 'The Land' which appears along with the story 'Friendly Brook' (1914) in the collection *A Diversity of Creatures* (1917). The poem tells the story of an estate symbolic of Britain as a whole, which is conquered and owned successively by Julius Fabricius, that is the Romans, Ogier the Dane, and William of Warenne, that is the Normans; then this land passes on to the narrator in the reign of George the Fifth. He is armed with 'title-deeds, attested, signed and sealed' which guarantee his complete rights over this land. However all through history the real person who has used this piece of land is Hobden, the Briton: he and his sons have tilled it. The problem of to whom this land really belongs comes to the fore when the landed proprietor thinks aloud:

> I have rights of chase and warren, as my dignity
>   requires.
> I can fish — but Hobden tickles. I can shoot — but
>   Hobden wires.
> I repair, but he reopens, certain gaps which, men allege,
> Have been used by every Hobden since a Hobden swapped
>   a hedge.
>
> (*DE* 603)

Hobden is guilty of poaching, and the proprietor can summon him 'to judgement', but he checks his anger:

> His dead are in the churchyard — thirty generations
>   laid. . . .
> And the passion and the piety and prowess of his line
> Have seeded, rooted, fruited in some land *the Law* calls
>   mine. . . .
> He is bailiff, woodman, wheelwright, field-surveyor,
>   engineer,
> And if flagrantly a poacher — 'tain't for me to interfere.
>
> (*DE* 603. Italics mine.)

Similarly the orders of a military authority may on occasion be refused. In 'A Centurion of the Thirtieth' (1906), included in *Puck of Pook's Hill*, Parnesius, a young officer, refuses to obey the order of the great general Maximus:

'Kill him now,' he [Maximus] said. 'He will not move a
limb.' 'No,' I said. 'You've taken my men out of my command. I should only be your butcher if I killed him now.'

(23 156)

These examples prove the fluidity of Kipling's concept of
Law, and one can multiply these examples indefinitely. However he makes it quite clear that the man-made Law (the law
of the land, military law, constitutional law and so forth) can
be modified, changed, disregarded and disobeyed in defer-
ence to a higher Law, which remains permanent and which
must be kept at all costs in all circumstances. This higher Law
is a necessity for the progress of civilization and the maintenance of the dignity of man. Dick Heldar in *The Light that
Failed* (1891) says that the Nilghai 'might have condensed
the whole of his lumbering nonsense into an epigram: "Only
the free are bond, and only the bond are free." ' (9 68–9) In
a tale in *The Jungle Books,* after Akela has been deposed
there is anarchy in the wolf-pack; but in due course, at the
meeting of the pack, one wolf cries out: 'Lead us again, O
Akela! Lead us again, O Man-cub, for we be sick of this
lawlessness, and we would be the Free People once more.' (7
134) In a later tale Akela exhorts the young wolves:
'. . . follow the Law, and run under one head, as befitted the
Free People.' (7 220)

Critics are in general agreement on the point that the Law
is a positive force, and that the final view of Kipling must be
based on a correct understanding of his Law. Nevertheless the
full and exact determination of the nature of Kipling's Law
remains an unsolved problem: so far as I am aware, no systematic and detailed study of this extremely important aspect
of Kipling has yet been undertaken.

A careful perusal of Kipling's works taken as an organic
unity reveals that his Law, the positive force with which he
opposes the Dark Forces, is composed of three main interrelated ingredients: moral values, the Imperial Idea and the
doctrine of disinterested suffering and positive action. The
purpose of this study is to investigate these three ingredients
of Law in order to determine the nature, value and validity of
this particular code of life, thereby filling a gap in Kipling
research. My solution may not be the best answer to the

problem. It will, however, interrelate various subthemes of Kipling's works which have been explored separately elsewhere, and it will attempt to weave the complex web of Kipling's thought into a new unity.

One may attack the problem of analysing an artist's philosophy in two ways. First, one may base one's investigations solely on the primary sources, isolated from the writer's biography as well as from the milieu in which those works are produced. This is a modern, new critical technique. The second is a much older method, namely the historical technique, which combines the study of the primary works with the background that went into the shaping and production of the works under examination.

Both techniques have value. However in the case of Rudyard Kipling, a writer endowed with what T. S. Eliot calls 'historical imagination',[10] and who 'composed', according to the tribute paid by *The Times* on Kipling's death, 'at a crucial period in the history of our race',[11] the historical approach is perhaps necessary if we are to arrive at a judicious understanding of his mind and art.

By proposing to adopt the historical approach in this study, I do not mean to uncover social, political, historical or biographical details each time that I refer to Kipling's works. Simply, I intend to place Kipling in the context of his times in order to view him from a proper perspective. Therefore in the course of this investigation, in addition to an examination of Kipling's works, I will touch upon those factors which contributed, directly or indirectly, to the formulation of Kipling's philosophy of Law.

C SUMMARY

Kipling is perhaps the most controversial figure in English literature. After a meteoric rise to fame, Kipling fell into disrepute around the turn of the century when he was generally dismissed as a jingo imperialist and a superficial writer. In 1941 T. S. Eliot's plea for consideration of Kipling as a major writer led to a revival of interest in Kipling as a craftsman. The efforts at a rehabilitation of Kipling as a consummate artist culminated in 1959 with the publication of J. M. S. Tompkins' *The Art of Rudyard Kipling*. In the meantime several defenses of Kipling's thought were also made, particularly by Bonamy Dobrée who called attention to the fact that Kipling was a writer of depth and vision. The representative critical essays of the last three decades collected by Andrew Rutherford in *Kipling's Mind and Art* (1964) and by Elliot L. Gilbert in *Kipling and the Critics* (1965) give a fair impression of a gradual shift in Kipling's position in the literary world since his death.

Nevertheless the controversy about Kipling's ideas is hardly over and 'the riddle of Kipling' is yet to be solved. The present study is an attempt at an understanding of Kipling's philosophy through an analysis of his frequently used term 'Law', which can be taken as the unitive principle around which the complex web of Kipling's thought is woven. A comprehensive determination of the nature of Kipling's Law has so far remained incomplete, although of course various subthemes of this concept have been explored individually before. Thus this study aims at filling a gap in Kipling research.

2 Aspects of Order and Law in Kipling's Formative Years

Yes . . . I will be a Burra Sahib Bahadur *(a very big man indeed)!*

'Baa Baa, Black Sheep' (6 327)

A 'A VERY YOUNG PERSON': BOMBAY AND SOUTHSEA (1865–78)

Kipling was born in Bombay in 1865 — a time when the British Empire in India was at its zenith. The Indo-Pakistani struggle for independence of 1857, which is referred to as 'the Mutiny' by English historians, was successfully quelled, and the Afghan wars, at least for the time being, were over. The country was going through a period of relative peace which it had not seen for centuries. Kipling's father, John Lockwood Kipling, enjoyed a secure prestige in British India as Professor of Architectural Sculpture at the Bombay School of Arts endowed by a public-spirited Parsee Sir Jamsetjee Jeejeebhoy.

'My first impression,' writes Kipling in *Something of Myself* (1937), 'is of daybreak, light and colour and purple fruits at the level of my shoulder. This would be the memory of early morning walks to the Bombay fruit market with my *ayah* (nurse) . . .' (36 3) The tender memories of the Bombay childhood spent 'between the palms and the sea' are easily discernible from his highly reticent autobiography. Little Ruddy was literally smothered by the love and affection of his father's Indian servants, especially Meeta and his *ayah,* a Goanese woman. The Indian influence was so deep that Hindustani or Urdu was 'the vernacular idiom one thought and dreamed in' and Ruddy spoke English 'haltingly translated out of the vernacular idiom.' (36 4)

Kipling's Bombay childhood is of immense importance in the development of his mind. In these six formative years he learnt and saw things which left an indelible mark, and later days were only to feed and water these half-formed ideas. One inevitable result of this period was the establishment of a tender bond between Kipling and India; this childhood bond never broke, and one can always perceive this sub-surface current of emotional involvement underneath his most bitter diatribes against India.

The second impression left on his personality by his Bombay childhood, later strengthened by what Kipling calls 'Seven Years' Hard' in India, was what I may term '*Sahib* consciousness'. Kipling was an intelligent child; he knew that he belonged to the ruling class; and perhaps he also understood what sort of person a *sahib* was supposed to be. André Chevrillon, one of Kipling's French admirers, paints the following imaginative but undoubtedly true picture of little Ruddy:

> Doubtless the child learns other things at Bombay, which leave a lasting impression. He sees the fine soldiers of the Queen; he sees the sepoys presenting arms to Europeans. He sees in the bazaars, around the temples and sacred ponds, the dark, half-naked crowd, making way for the Englishman's horse. He sees the *salaams,* the hands laid on heart, lips, and bending brow. Surely the child is aware that he belongs to the ruling race — his nurse or his bearer must have told him that he is a *sahib.* And may be he has already formed some idea of the duties and the honour of a *sahib.* [1]

André Chevrillon's picture is confirmed by the following scene of a leave-taking between young Kipling and his Indian servants in the deeply autobiographical story 'Baa Baa, Black Sheep' (1888):

> 'Come back, Punch-*baba*,' said the *ayah.*
> 'Come back,' said Meeta, 'and be a *Burra Sahib* (a big man).'
> 'Yes,' said Punch, lifted up in his father's arms to wave good-bye. 'Yes, I will come back, and I will be a *Burra Sahib Bahadur* (a very big man indeed)!'
>
> (6 327)

Many of Kipling's stories project this image of himself as a *chota sahib* or 'child of the Dominant Race', strong-willed, imperious and conscious of a profound sense of responsibility. For example 'Wee Willie Winkie' (1888) is a story of six-year-old Willie, who was also 'an officer and a gentleman'. (6 287) He understood 'what Military Discipline meant' (6 287), he had been brought up to believe that 'tears were the depth of unmanliness' (6 298), and he possessed all the qualities of a *sahib* — authority, honour, heroism, discipline and a sense of superiority.

When Miss Allardyce, the girlfriend of Coppy who is a friend of Willie and a subaltern in his father's regiment, rides toward the river bordering the free tribal territory, young Willie gallops to her succour. He overtakes her near the river where they are encircled by the fierce Pathans. Willie is not afraid: 'Then rose from the rock Wee Willie Winkee, child of the Dominant Race, aged six and three-quarters, and said briefly and emphatically, ' *"Jao!"* (go).' Ultimately the Pathans disappear into the hills; the regiment of Willie's father comes in search and Coppy exclaims: ' "You're a hero, Winkie — a *pukka* [true] hero!" ' (6 304)

The happy period of Bombay childhood is pictured in several stories. In 'Tods' Amendment' (1887) little Tods is shown as 'the idol of some eighty *jhampanis* [porters], and half as many *saises* [grooms]. . . . It never entered his head that any living human being could disobey his orders'. (1 218)

But this golden period in Bombay came to an end all too soon. Kipling and his younger sister Trix, who were then about six and three years old respectively, were sent to Southsea, England, as paying guests in the home of a retired naval officer whose name had been obtained from an advertisement in a newspaper and who seemed to have satisfactory references!

The five years' stay at Lorne Lodge, Southsea, left deep scars upon the spirit of Kipling; one may form a vague notion of his experiences at 'The House of Desolation' from *Something of Myself,* 'Baa Baa, Black Sheep' (1888) and the first chapter of his novel *The Light that Failed* (1890). Here is an excerpt from his autobiography telling something of the miseries and hardships which he suffered at the hands of the religious tyrant, Mrs Holloway:

It was an establishment run with the full vigour of the Evangelical as revealed to the Woman. I had never heard of Hell, so I was introduced to it in all its terrors — I and whatever luckless little slavey might be in the house, whom severe rationing had led to steal food. Once I saw the Woman beat such a girl who picked up the kitchen poker and threatened retaliation. Myself I was regularly beaten. The Woman had an only son of twelve or thirteen as religious as she. I was a real joy to him, for when his mother had finished with me for the day he (we slept in the same room) took me on and roasted the other side.

(36 7–8)

'Baa Baa, Black Sheep' is a bitter work. At a very tender age, the golden world of 'daybreak, light and colour and purple fruits' had disappeared, and instead all hell was let loose:

When a matured man discovers that he has been deserted by Providence, deprived of his God, and cast without help, comfort, or sympathy, upon a world which is new and strange to him, his despair, which may find expression in evil living, the writing of his experiences, or the more satisfactory diversion of suicide, is generally supposed to be impressive. A child, under exactly similar circumstances as far as its knowledge goes, cannot very well curse God and die. It howls till its nose is red, its eyes are sore, and its head aches. Punch and Judy, through no fault of their own, had lost all their world.

(6 333)

The effects of these agonizing years at Lorne Lodge have, however, been unduly exaggerated and misconstrued, especially by those interested in psychoanalysis. To say, as for example Edmund Wilson does, that as a result of them 'the whole work of Kipling's life is to be shot through with hatred'[2] is quite unjustified.

One should read Kipling's comments on the effects of these sad experiences with care in order to form a correct opinion of the impact of these years on his personality and art. In 'Baa Baa, Black Sheep' Kipling states: 'When young

lips have drunk deep of the bitter waters of Hate, Suspicion,
and Despair, all the Love in the world will not wholly take
away that knowledge; though it may turn darkened eyes for a
while to the light, and teach Faith where no Faith was.' (6
368) In *Something of Myself* he goes on to say: 'In the long
run these things, and many more of the like, drained me of
any capacity for real, personal hate for the rest of my days.
So close must any life-filling passion lie to its opposite.' (36
17) In these related statements Kipling makes two points:
first, his early knowledge of hatred, suspicion and despair;
second, the resultant incapacity for any personal feeling of
hate and a preoccupation with the opposite of hate, that is,
pity and love. Thus the theme of hatred and revenge is
accompanied by the theme of compassion, healing and love
in his works.[3]

One consequence of the young Kipling's exile was that it
made him see authority from a new angle. The child Ruddy
who wielded authority in India and who was petted and
loved by his father's Indian servants was now bullied and
ordered about by a religious tyrant. The circle was completed, and the bitter though of course valuable lesson of
obedience to authority was driven home.

B 'THE SCHOOL BEFORE ITS TIME': UNITED SERVICES COLLEGE (1878–82)

The four years (1878–82) which Kipling spent at United
Services College, popularly known as Westward Ho!, further
contributed to the inculcation of certain basic elements of
what was to become his philosophy of Law.

United Services College was established by Army officers
as a cheap training ground for their sons who were assumed
to be gentlemen and who were qualifying for entrance to the
imperial service. An interesting advertisement in *The Illustrated London News* of 23 January 1875 says this about the
school:

> The object of the United Services Proprietary College at
> Westward Ho is to provide for the sons of the officers of
> the Army and Navy an inexpensive education of the
> highest class and of a general nature. It is also to prepare

them for the military, naval, and civil examinations, or for the universities, or for the liberal professions, or for mercantile and general pursuits.

The following excerpt from the 'Editorial Notes' of *The United Services College Chronicle* throws further light on the end to which the school was directed:

> In July next, the College comes of age, and we confidently call on all her sons, past and present, to make the year 1895, a memorable one in the annals of the school. In twenty years the College has made its way in the school world, and earned a place among the Public Schools of England. We hope that the year will be marked by successes in the class rooms, and on the playing fields, and that we may continue to turn out, in the words of Lord Roberts, quoted by Mr. Rudyard Kipling, 'a good, efficient and trustworthy type of officer.'[4]

Life at Westward Ho! was ordered and masculine, and like the other English public schools of the time, generally speaking, was geared to the turning out of the officers for the Empire with qualities of courage, endurance, firmness of character, strength of will, sense of superiority of the English over others and so forth.[5]

While at school Kipling did not shine in sports, but he edited the college magazine and was active in the 'Literary and Debating Society', which was formed in November 1881 with Kipling as Secretary. Dunsterville, ('Stalky'), one of his intimate friends, was elected President. There were poetry readings, and debates on such issues as 'the present Government is unworthy of the confidence of the country' (Gladstone was in power at that time); 'the advance of the Russians in Central Asia is hostile to the British Power'; 'total abstinence is better than the moderate use of alcohol' — and so on: Kipling being invariably for the motion.[6]

The spirit infused by the United Services College in Kipling and other students is well reflected by 'Ave Imperatrix!' — a poem which Kipling wrote on the occasion of the attempt to assassinate Queen Victoria in March 1882:

One school of many made to make
　　Men who shall hold it dearest right
To battle for their ruler's sake,
　　And stake their being in the fight,

Sends greeting humble and sincere —
　　Though verse be rude and poor and mean —
To you, the greatest as most dear —
　　Victoria, by God's grace Our Queen!

Such greeting as should come from those
　　Whose fathers faced the Sepoy hordes,
Or served you in the Russian snows,
　　And, dying, left their sons their swords.

And some of us have fought for you
　　Already in the Afghan pass —
Or where the scarce-seen smoke-puffs flew
　　From Boer marksmen in the grass;

And all are bred to do your will
　　By land and sea — wherever flies
The Flag, to fight and follow still,
　　And work your Empire's destinies.

(DE 169)

In *Stalky & Co.* (1899) Kipling painted an exaggerated picture of his school days at Westward Ho!, but from this book one can form some impression of the Spartan atmosphere that prevailed there. The atmosphere of the book is charged with violence. Stalky, the central figure, is projected as the ideal product of this system as he turns out to be an excellent Empire-builder — something which he owes to the discipline and the philosophy of action learnt at school:

Out of Egypt unto Troy —
　　Over Himalaya
Far and sure our bands have gone —
　　Hy-Brasil or Babylon,
Islands of the Southern Run,
　　And cities of Cathaia! . . .

> This we learned from famous men,
>   Knowing not its uses,
> When they showed, in daily work —
> Man must finish off his work —
> Right or wrong, his daily work —
>   And without excuses. . . .
>
> This we learned from famous men
>   Teaching in our borders,
> Who declared it was best,
> Safest, easiest, and best —
> Expeditious, wise, and best —
>   To obey your orders.
>
> (18 viii–ix)

C 'SEVEN YEARS' HARD': INDIA (1882–9)

A tablet in Kipling's Lahore office asserts that 'here I "worked" ', and in *Something of Myself* he goes on to add 'And Allah knows that is true also!' (36 74) 'Seven Years' Hard' — the title of the chapter on his Indian period in his autobiography — is another indication of some aspects of his life in India which are of particular relevance to this study. Hard, ceaseless work seems to be the keynote of his youthful years in India:

> I never worked less than ten hours and seldom more than fifteen per diem; and as our paper came out in the evening did not see the midday sun except on Sundays. I had fever too, regular and persistent, to which I added for a while chronic dysentery. Yet I discovered that a man can work with a temperature of 104, even though next day he has to ask the office who wrote the article. . . . From the modern point of view I suppose the life was not fit for a dog, but my world was filled with boys, but a few years older than I, who had lived utterly alone, and died from typhoid mostly at the regulation age of twenty-two. As regarding ourselves at home, if there were any dying to be done, we four were together. The rest was in the day's work . . .
>
> (36 40–1)

In a letter of 17 November 1882, one of the earliest he
wrote on arrival in Lahore, addressed to one of his teachers at
Westward Ho!, he talks about the heavy work at the *Civil &
Military Gazette* office for which he alone was responsible —
putting together the bulk of the paper, proof-reading, report-
ing, and skimming through some thirty odd local and foreign
newspapers daily.[7] Kipling worked there under Stephen
Wheeler, the two comprising the entire editorial staff of a
paper that kept sixty native compositors at work.[8] On his
transfer to the *Pioneer* of Allahabad in 1887 the pressure of
work did not diminish, for then he alone was responsible for
the editing and writing of the *Pioneer Mail* and the *Week's
News,* two off-print papers of the *Pioneer.*

Kipling's devotion to work was partly inspired by the
example of his father, John Lockwood Kipling. Lockwood
Kipling was no imperialist; he was a solid, genial, practical,
hard-working craftsman with an encyclopedic knowledge of
many aspects of Indian life. It was because of the good work
he had done in Bombay that in 1872 he was promoted to
curator of the Lahore Museum and principal of the then
newly-founded Mayo School of Arts, Lahore. The grey-
bearded curator of the Lahore Museum in *Kim* (who is
modelled after Lockwood Kipling) is Kipling's own testi-
mony of the diligence and scholarship of his father.

At this stage, as pointed out by Louis Cornell, Kipling also
realized that in work alone lay the salvation of the Anglo-
Indian community.[9] The India of the eighties was very different from the India of the sixties and the seventies. By this
time an English-educated Indian middle-class intelligentsia
had firmly appeared on the scene, and it aspired to establish a
new order. On his arrival in India, Kipling found himself, to
use Noel Annan's words, amidst 'a society which politically,
nervously, physically, and spiritually quivered on the edge of
a precipice.'[10] The storm was to gather its full strength later;
but Kipling with an artist's keen perceptions was quick to
assess the emergence of the new forces. He hastened to
oppose the nationalist movement in India for, right or wrong,
he felt that (a) Indians could not stand on their own feet, at
that time at least, and (b) Indians were in greater need of
basic facilities than of democracy. Thus he advocated that

the Anglo-Indians must do hard, selfless work in order to justify their presence in India and elsewhere.

Kipling's conviction about the need for practical work in India rather than abstract discussions regarding democracy was based on his intimate knowledge of India and its problems. Journalism gave him ample opportunity to examine the Indian scene closely, an experience which was crucial to the development of his philosophy of life. This is how he described the kind of work he was engaged in at Lahore:

> I was sent out, first for local reportings ... Later I described openings of big bridges and such-like, which meant a night or two with the engineers; floods on railways — more nights in the wet with wretched heads of repair gangs; village festivals and consequent outbreaks of cholera or small pox; communal riots under the shadow of the Mosque of Wazir Khan, where the patient waiting troops lay in timber-yards ... visits of Viceroys to neighbouring Princes on the edge of the great Indian Desert, ... reviews of Armies expecting to move against Russia next week; receptions of an Afghan Potentate, with whom the Indian Government wished to stand well ... murder and divorce trials ...
>
> (36 43-4)

This passage gives an idea of the range of Kipling's movements and activities as a journalist. He acquainted himself with people from almost all walks of life — soldiers at Mian Mir Cantonment; engineers, doctors, civil servants, planters, and merchants at the Panjab Club; and 'Muslims, Hindus, Sikhs, and members of the Arya and Brahmo Smaj' at the Masonic Lodge.

As regards the Anglo-Indian life, Simla gave him profound insight into the social life of his own people — the people who controlled the 'naked machinery' of the Indian Government. The problems of the country were therefore understood by him in a way never done before by any other western artist writing about India. Instead of painting a hackneyed romantic picture of India, Kipling presented the real India — that vast chaotic country crawling with life — so much of which was diseased or decaying, torn with racial hatreds and racked with ear-splitting discords. It seemed to him that it was only through the Empire, in which he perceived traces of the Imperial Idea, that some order could be established over the general chaos. As far as he was concerned any notion of the crumbling of the Empire's magnificient machinery and of the return of power to the Indians meant a return to chaos. This point will be fully illustrated in the pages to follow; here I shall confine myself to giving an example from his journalistic writings of the period.

In 1888 Kipling was sent to Calcutta by the *Pioneer* to report on the functioning of the local self-government over there. On entering the city, the first thing he noticed was the smell that permeated every corner of the town. The Indian councillors were busy discussing J. S. Mill and democratic values while Kipling worried about cleaning up the city: 'Where is the criminal, and what is all this talk about abstractions? They want shovels, not sentiments, in this part of the world.'[11] 'Shovels, not sentiments' gives the key to Kipling's attitude of mind.

A long essay on the 1888 meeting of the Indian National Congress, then in its third year, leaves no doubt about his point of view. As Louis Cornell remarks, Kipling ridicules the Congress by observing that they were incapable of conducting an orderly meeting, let alone the affairs of the subcontinent. In a letter to his friend H. A. Gwynne written towards the end of his life, he clarifies why he was opposed to the Congress:

> Within one year of the establishment of any sort of unchecked 'national' administration there will be *suttee* again, dacoity there is already in full flow. Very few of the political movements and *hartals* [strikes] are unaccompanied by robbery, house breaking or murderous assaults. . . . I only want to save as many lives as are possible.[12]

In another letter to Gwynne, Kipling sheds further light on the subject:

> A large proportion of the 'educated' Hindus would accept some form of 'westernized' government to save their 'face'. The outcome of that, of course, would be oppression, ex-

tortion, and the sale of justice rather more than at present, and an even greater collapse of municipal administration than exists today.[13]

While one may not like Kipling's anti-liberal stance, one must admit that these examples show Kipling's down to earth, practical approach to the Indian problems: he was more concerned with taking prompt action in order to alleviate the lot of the man in the street than giving him the right to govern himself. Hero-worship such as he had given to his friends at Westward Ho! now went to ordinary men like Findlayson, Strickland or Hummil who toiled in remote corners of the Empire for the betterment of India's 'brown and naked humanity'. A profound sense of moral responsibility, a need of hard and selfless work and a faith in the Empire were the direct results of his experiences in India. It was during the 'Seven Years' Hard' in India that consciously or unconsciously Kipling formed the sympathies which developed into his creed of the 'Law'.

In March 1889 Kipling left India for ever, and he was to spend the greater part of the rest of his life as a gypsy wandering all over the world. Of the seventy years of his life, Kipling spent only thirteen in India, but the fact remains that those thirteen left a deeper mark on his mind and art than the fifty-seven years spent in England, the United States, South Africa, and France. Those fifty-seven years only confirmed the views that he had formed during his stay in India: strong beliefs in positive action, in law and order and in the Empire remained the keynotes of his post-Indian career.

D SUMMARY

We have seen that the foundation of Kipling's philosophy of Law was laid in the first twenty-five years of his life. The Bombay Childhood (1865—71) was directly responsible for what I have termed *sahib*-consciousness — an awareness that one belongs to the ruling class, a belief in authority, and a sense of responsibility. The painful years at Southsea (1871—78) made him see authority from the new angle of obedience and submission. A strong patriotism, enthusiasm for the Empire, discipline and the doctrine of work were inculcated in him during his stay at United Services College,

Westward Ho! (1878—82). The next seven years which he spent in India as a journalist were crucial to the development of his ideas, providing him with a unique opportunity to understand India, its problems and the way these problems were handled by British rulers.

In fact, it was during his 'Seven Years' Hard' in India that consciously or unconsciously Kipling formed the sympathies which developed into a creed that he termed the Law. And it was because of his experiences in India, as it will be made clear in the following pages, that he became a firm advocate of a moral code, the Imperial Idea and the Doctrine of Action — the three bases of his Law.

3 The Moral Order

This matter of creeds is like horse-flesh. The wise man knows horses are good — that there is a profit to be made from all. . . . Therefore I say in my heart the Faiths are like the horses. Each has merit in its own country.

19 234

A GROUNDWORK IN RELIGION

Realisation of a moral order is postulated by Kipling as the first step in the struggle against the Forces of Chaos and Disorder. In fact his vision of a moral order, consisting of such universal values as discipline, devotion to work, positive action, suffering and love, forms the very basis of his philosophy of Law.

This conception of a universal moral order was largely a result of his experiences in India — the land of diverse castes and creeds. It was here that he was exposed to various religious and philosophic systems, and he realised that they were all concerned with one common object, namely, the moral and spiritual well-being of man. This perception of a common denominator among diverse religions confirmed his faith in the hidden and veiled Power that is working against the Dark Powers in its own mysterious ways. So he naturally came to respect all religions, whether Christian, Muslim, Hindus, Sikhs, and members of the Arya and Brahmo Smaj' at the Masonic Lodge.

> O ye who tread the Narrow Way
> By Tophet-flare to Judgement Day,
> Be gentle when "the heathen" pray
> To Buddha at Kamakura! . . .
>
> And whoso will, from Pride released,
> Contemning neither creed nor priest,
> May feel the Soul of all the East
> About him at Kamakura. . . .

The poem ends with a satirical gesture at the materialistic Western tourist:

> A tourist-show, a legend told,
> A rusting bulk of bronze and gold,
> So much, and scarce so much, ye hold
> The meaning of Kamakura?
>
> But when the morning prayer is prayed,
> Think, ere ye pass to strife and trade,
> Is God in human image made
>   No nearer than Kamakura?
>   (*DE* 92–3)

Even the worship of Hanuman should be respected: the moral of the story 'The Mark of the Beast' (1890) is 'Don't trifle with the beliefs of other people'. Mahbub Ali puts this message succinctly for Kipling when he says to Kim: ' "This matter of creeds is like horse-flesh. The wise man knows horses are good — that there is a profit to be made from all . . . Therefore I say in my heart the Faiths are like the horses. Each has merit in its own country." ' (19 234)

Kipling was familiar with the great religions of the world. In this chapter I propose to examine the influence of these various religions on Kipling in order to understand the background that led to the formulation of his vision of a universal moral order. No discussion of Kipling's philosophy of Law can be complete without a consideration of the impact of diverse religions on him, for the moral side of Kipling's Law is related to the moral codes or ethical values recommended by these faiths.

B THE JUDAEO-CHRISTIAN TRADITION IN KIPLING'S WORK

One of the most striking aspects of Kipling's work is his constant quotation from the Bible, allusion to its stories and use of its language. This intimacy with the Bible was perfectly natural for him as both his grandfathers had been Wesleyan ministers and he must have heard much Biblical reference at home. The influence of the religious tyrant — Mrs Holloway — at the 'House of Desolation' must also be taken into account. Afternoons upstairs with the Collects or portions of the Bible to memorise provided him with an endless fund of texts upon which to draw. (36 12) And then there were the services at school. With his sensitivity for language, he remembered and repeated biblical words and phrases. A mere glance at his titles proves the point. *Many Inventions, Thy Servant a Dog,* 'Bread upon the Waters', 'The Prophet and the Country', 'The Church that was at Antioch', 'Delilah', 'The Sons of Martha',[1] and so forth.

Apart from book and story titles, Kipling's works are full of biblical quotations and allusions.[2] The wording is rarely exact, but the source is unmistakable. Here are a few examples: 'Gentlemen-Rankers': 'The curse of Reuben holds us'. (*DE* 425) — The actual curse is: 'Unstable as water, thou shalt not excel.' (Genesis 49:4) 'Rhyme of the Three Sealers': 'Yea, skin for skin and all that he hath a man will give for his life.' (*DE* 116) — 'Skin for skin, yea, all that a man hath will he give for his life.' (Job 2:4) 'Islanders': 'No doubt but ye are the people.' (*DE* 301) — 'No doubt but ye are the people.' (Job 12:2) 'McAndrew's Hymn': ' *"Better the sight of eyes that see than wanderin' o' desire!"* ' (*DE* 123) — 'Better is the sight of the eyes than the wanderings of the desire.' (Ecclesiastes 6:9)

So one might go on. Kipling draws from almost every book in the Bible. There is hardly any incident in the Gospels which is not referred to in his works. Job, the Psalms and Isaiah were his preferred readings among the poetical books, and all the books of wisdom — Proverbs, Ecclesiastes, and the Apocryphal Ecclesiasticus — are frequently cited. Although proportionately the books of the law and the minor prophets are not so often referred to as the lyrical and proverbial ones, altogether Kipling's writings reveal a deeper influence of the Old Testament spirit than that of the New Testament. Out of some 671 allusions which have been traced to chapter and book in Kipling's works, 418 are to the Old Testament, 253 to the New; moreover there are numerous passages in which Kipling falls into biblical language, and here his cadences are generally those of the Old Testament, the King James Authorized Version of 1611.[3]

The concept of divine law, so important in the literature of

the Old Testament, definitely contributed to the formulation
of Kipling's philosophy of Law. While the Jewish sacred writings were divided into three parts known respectively as the
law, the prophets and the writings, it was the first of these, or
what came to be known as the Book of the Law, that took
precedence over the other two groups. The Law was regarded
not only as the most important but as the most inspired of all
the Old Testament writings. It was for this reason that the
Hebrew religion has frequently been characterised as legalistic: it is highly moral and prescriptive. Yahweh, the source
of all law, is an all-powerful and rather angry deity whose
command is perceived as active and dynamic by analogy to
the command which a general exercises over his army. The
emphasis in biblical law falls heavily upon order, authority,
discipline, responsibility and a primitive kind of justice. The
primary purpose of this law is to regulate the life of the
community and order the relationship of the community
with God.

The impact of the biblical law on Kipling is well reflected
in his attitude towards life and especially in the nomism of
The Jungle Books (see Chapter 6). However Kipling's view of
morality cannot be dismissed as legalistic, for he does postu-
late an end to be realised rather than merely a law to be
fulfilled. This end is, as will be made clear in the pages to
follow, the destruction of the Forces of Disorder and Darkness.

Christian ethics, alike in its Protestant and Catholic forms,
has always upheld the conception of law and rejected anti-
nomianism, that is the doctrine that the moral agent who has
attained to maturity has no need of external ordinances. On
the other hand Christianity has made a special effort to guard
against what may be called positive legalism, which forgets
that law and obedience are merely the forms of the moral life
and not its substance.

In the Christian tradition the Wesleyan doctrine of vocation may have excercised some influence on the development
of Kipling's philosophy of life for he had a nonconformist
background. Wesleyan Methodism exalted work as the dis-
tinguishing feature of moral character. Therefore, it was
pointed out: 'Every man that has any pretence to be a
Christian' will not fail to school himself rigorously to 'the

business' of his calling, 'seeing it is impossible that an idle man can be a good man, — sloth being inconsistent with religion'.[4] Wesley advanced the dogma that 'without industry we are neither fit for this world, nor for the world to come'.[5] 'To show all possible diligence,' declared Wesley, 'is one of our standing rules; and one, concerning the observance of which we continually make the strictest inquiry.'[6] This glorification of work was a keynote of a comprehensive attitude towards life. Idleness was actually ranked with the most heinous crimes. The business of life was a serious affair, for no part of it lay outside the divine purpose. The Wesleyan movement almost invariably addressed itself to practical problems.[7] It is therefore not unreasonable to assume that Kipling's Doctrine of Action and his moral earnestness are related to his nonconformist background. (See Chapter 5 for a full discussion of Kipling's gospel of work.)

The Christian values of suffering and love find expression in Kipling's later works, revealing how deeply he was influenced by this facet of the Christian message. For example the protagonists of two important fables — 'The Children of the Zodiac' (1891) and 'Cold Iron' (1909) — come down to earth from heaven and fairy-land, identify themselves completely with suffering humanity, and take upon their shoulders the mundane work and burdens of mankind out of sheer love in order to alleviate the lot of man. (Also see Chapter 5, Section A.)

The poem 'Cold Iron', which accompanies the story of the same title, brings out explicitly the values of suffering and of sacrificial love. The poem tells of a Baron (who seems to represent Man) taken prisoner for rebellion against the King, apparently Christ. The Baron blames Cold Iron, which is symbolic of stern necessity or fate, for his fall, and he asserts that the King does not know what Cold Iron means. Then the King tells the Baron how he himself experienced Cold Iron when he went down to earth to redeem fallen Man:

'See! These Hands they pierced with nails, outside
　My city wall,
Show Iron — Cold Iron — to be master of men all. . . .
I forgive thy treason — I redeem thy fall —
For Iron — Cold Iron — must be master of men all!'
(*DE* 509)

The reference here is obviously to the Crucifixion. Through this powerful Christian symbol, the poem sets forth the value that Kipling places on disinterested suffering and sacrificial love.

The same message is conveyed in 'A Carol', which accompanies the story 'The Tree of Justice' (1910), where Harold of England is shown, still alive after the Norman Conquest, a broken old man even as the tree is broken in the poem:

> Our Lord Who did the Ox command
>   To kneel to Judah's King,
> He binds His frost upon the land
>   To ripen it for Spring —
> To ripen it for Spring, good sirs,
>   According to His Word. . . .
>
> When we poor fenmen skate the ice
>   Or shiver on the wold,
> We hear the cry of a single tree
>   That breaks her heart in the cold —
> That breaks her heart in the cold, good sirs,
>   And rendeth by the board. . . .
>
> Her wood is crazed and little worth
>   Excepting as to burn,
> That we may warm and make our mirth
>   Until the Spring return —.
>
> (*DE* 510–11)

The single tree, a victim of the frost, is an unavoidable sacrifice to the great good of preparing the people for the spring: in the same way old Harold is sacrificed to the greater good of preparing for the growth of a mighty nation.

Another story in which the Christian note is unmistakable is 'The Gardener' (1926), the last story in *Debits and Credits*. Helen Turrell has had an illegitimate son, Michael, whom she has passed off as her nephew. Michael is killed in the war, and at the end of the story Helen visits the war cemetery where he is buried. She is, however, unable to locate the grave, and looks around for help:

A man knelt behind a line of headstones — evidently a gardener, for he was firming a young plant in the soft earth. She went towards him, her paper in her hand. He rose at her approach and without prelude or salutation asked: 'Who are you looking for?'

'Lieutenant Michael Turrell — my nephew,' said Helen slowly and word for word, as she had many thousands of times in her life.

The man lifted his eyes and looked at her with infinite compassion before he turned from the fresh-sown grass toward the naked black crosses.

'Come with me,' he said, 'and I will show you where your son lies.'

When Helen left the Cemetery she turned for a last look. In the distance she saw the man bending over his young plants; and she went away, supposing him to be the gardener.

(31 449-50)

The story will make its full impact only if we recognise the reference to St John's Gospel (20:15) in which Mary Magdalene goes to the tomb to find the body of Jesus, and the man there who speaks to her she supposes to be a gardener. This story indicates, as Professor Dobrée remarks, that Kipling's hope of, if not faith in, infinite mercy was one of the supports by the aid of which he lived.[8]

Similarly the light-hearted fantasy 'On the Gate' (1926) is a vision of mercy, not judgment. Here we see St Peter holding the keys of Heaven, and dedicating himself to an endless exercise of mercy. He is entirely concerned with compassionate forgiveness for mankind so that they may enter Heaven rather than be consigned to the 'Lower Establishment' (Hell). The story is, however, touched with satire. It is set in Heaven which is described in terms of the machinery of an earthly governmental department, for 'the Order Above' is 'but the reflection of the Order Below'. Peter appears as an efficient civil servant; he is administratively preoccupied with alloting people their various categories: ' "Good!" St Peter rubbed his hands. "That brings her under the higher allowance — G.L.H. scale — "Greater love hath no man —." ' (31 361) While this story brings out Kipling's disbelief in dogmatic Christianity, it also brings the Christian teaching down to earth and translates it into realistic practical concerns.

Kipling, it must be remarked, was not strictly speaking a professing Christian. Though responsive to Christian ethical ideals, and imaginatively responsive to such things as village churches, characters of saints and so forth, though he uses Christian symbols seriously (in 'Cold Iron', 'The Gardener', etc.), and though his work is full of biblical quotations and allusions, there is in fact very little evidence anywhere in Kipling's writings of an adherence to articles of Christian faith. 'The Gardener' is the only story which has a positive reference to Christ.

Indeed there is much to show that no formal, organised Christian faith would have satisfied him.[9] In an early letter (9 December 1889) to Caroline Taylor, the daughter of a clergyman to whom Kipling paid court while he was visiting the United States of America, he confesses:

> Your slave was baptised in Bombay Cathedral into the Church of England, which you call Episcopalian, was brought up as you have read in that church, and confirmed by the Bishop of Exeter in Bideford Church, in '80 or '81. Does that satisfy that I am not a veiled adherent of the Church of Rome? ... I believe in the existence of a personal God to whom we are personally responsible for wrongdoing — that it is our duty to follow and our peril to disobey the ten ethical laws laid down for us by Him and His prophets. I disbelieve directly in eternal punishment, for reasons that would take too long to put down on paper. On the same grounds I disbelieve in an eternal reward. As regards the mystery of the Trinity and the Doctrine of Redemption, I regard them most reverently but I cannot give them implicit belief.[10]

In another letter (16 October 1895) he expresses his dissatisfaction with Christianity and Christians:

> It is my fortune to have been born and to a large extent brought up among those whom white men call 'heathen'; and while I recognise the paramount duty of every white man to follow the teaching of his creed and conscience as

'a debtor to the whole law', it seems to me cruel that white men, whose governments are armed with the most murderous weapons known to science, should amaze and confound their fellow creatures with a doctrine of salvation imperfectly understood by themselves and a code of ethics foreign to the climate and instincts of those races whose most cherished customs they outrage and whose gods they insult.[11]

In the early stories he is content to imply that Christianity could well be explained simply as a stage in evolution and no more.[12] And frequently his attitude towards Christianity is satirical to say the least: 'On the Gate' (see above) is a ready example.

Thus we see that Kipling makes much use of the Bible, especially the Old Testament, and is influenced by biblical law, but he shows little adherence to formal Christianity and is in fact quite sardonic in his references to the Christian religion in practice.

C THE ISLAMIC TRADITION IN KIPLING'S WORK

Kipling's works are interspersed with references to Islam, Allah, the Prophet Mohammed, the Koran, Islamic ethics, and Muslim literature and folklore. For example, the Introduction to the 'Outward Bound Edition' of his collected works begins with the well-known koranic verse: 'In the name of God the Compassionate, the Merciful.' (Koran 1, 1) This Introduction is in the form of a letter from the owner of the merchandise (that is, Kipling) to the *Nakhoda* (Persian for 'skipper') of the vessel, which is carrying the rich cargo (that is, Kipling's works) to the Western ports. The writer prays to Allah for the success of this venture: 'On Bhao Malung we pray before the voyage; at the Takaria Musjid we give thanks when the voyage is over.' (1, x) Similarly Kipling begins his autobiography, his final book, in the name of Allah: 'Therefore, ascribing all good fortune to Allah the Dispenser of Events, I begin:—.' (36 3)

The story 'The Enemies to Each Other' (1924) has a distinct Islamic atmosphere. The narrator Abu Ali Jafir Bin Yakub-ul-Isfahani tells the story of the creation of Adam.

When the Archangel Jibrail went to bring from the earth the substance that would make Adam, the earth 'shook and lamented and supplicated', and Jibrail, being moved by the laments, refrained as did the Archangel Michael. But the Archangel Azrael tore out the necessary sands and clays. When asked why he did not spare the earth he answered: ' "Obedience (to Thee) was more obligatory than Pity (for it)." ' Whence it was ordained that Azrael should become the Angel of Death. Azrael was further ordered to mix the clays and sands and lay them to dry between 'Tayif and Mecca' till the time appointed. And when the Soul unwillingly went through the agony of entering the body and the event was accomplished, 'the Word came: "My Compassion exceedeth My Wrath." ' These words recall 'The Lord is quick in retribution, but He is also Oft-forgiving, Most Merciful.' (Koran 7, 168—9) The story is a good example of Kipling's use of Islamic tradition.

Kipling's special use of Muslim literature and history is illustrated by several poems and stories. For instance he refers to Saadi, a famous Persian mystic and poet, in 'One View of the Question' (1890):

> And ye know what Saadi saith:—
> 'How may the merchant westward fare
> When he hears the tale of tumults there?'
> (6 284)

'The Rupaiyat of Omar Kal'vin' (1886) and 'Certain Maxims of Hafiz' (1886) indicate his familiarity with Omar Khayyam (at first no doubt through Fitzgerald's translation) and Hafiz Shirazi — two of the most celebrated classical Persian poets. There are also numerous references in his works to *The Arabian Nights*. As regards Muslim history, there are many references to Moghul emperors in particular: 'Akbar's Bridge' (1930) and 'The Amir's Homily' (1891) are ready examples.

Kipling's attitude towards Islam may be gathered from an early story 'The City of Dreadful Night' (1885). Here Kipling paints an impressionistic picture of Lahore on a hot and humid night in August. He approaches the city from a distance and gradually focuses his lens on the objects of his special interest. We get a bird's eye view of the city — the roof-tops, as far as one can see, are crammed with restless men, women and children, and the sleepers by the roadside look like corpses in the eerie moonlight. The entire city seems to be in the grip of the Dark Powers whose evil influence is ultimately broken by the call of a *Muezzin* (Muslim crier who calls the hour of daily prayers):

> 'Allah ho Akbar'; then a pause while another *Muezzin* somewhere in the direction of the Golden Temple takes up the call — 'Allah ho Akbar.' Again and again; four times in all; and from the bedsteads a dozen men have risen up already. — 'I bear witness that there is no God but God.' What a splendid cry it is, the proclamation of the creed that brings men out of their beds by scores at midnight! Once again he thunders through the same phrase, shaking with the vehemence of his voice; and then, far and near, the night air rings with 'Mahomed is the Prophet of God'. It is as though he were flinging his defiance to the far-off horizon, where the summer lightning plays and leaps like a bared sword.
>
> (4 42–3)

In 'Egypt of the Magicians' (1913), a record of his impressions of his visit to Egypt, he writes:

> Christian churches may compromise with images and side-chapels where the unworthy or abashed can traffic with accessible saints. Islam has but one pulpit and one stark affirmation — living or dying, one only — and where men have repeated that in red-hot belief through centuries, the air still shakes to it.
>
> (28 274)

Speaking about Islam in general, Kipling declares:

> Some men are Mohammedan by birth, some by training, and some by fate, but I have never met an Englishman yet who hated Islam and its people as I have met Englishmen who hated some other faiths. *Mussalmani awadani,* as the saying goes — where there are Mohammedans, there is a comprehensible civilisation.
>
> (28 274)

Describing his impressions of Al-Azhar — the thousand-year-old University of Cairo — he comments on the Koran-oriented curriculum of the university:

> The students sit on the ground, and their teachers instruct them, mostly by word of mouth, in grammar, syntax, logic; *al-hisab,* which is arithmetic; *al-jab'r w'al muqablah,* which is algebra; *at-tafsir,* commentaries on the Koran; and, last and most troublesome, *al-ahadis,* traditions, and yet more commentaries on the law of Islam, which leads back, like everything, to the Koran once again. (For it is written, 'Truly the Quran is none other than a revelation.') It is a very comprehensive curriculum.
>
> (28 275)

Kipling felt at home in the Muslim world: the Panjab where he spent five youthful years was predominantly a Muslim area. 'My life had lain among Muslims', he writes in his autobiography, 'and a man leans one way or other according to his first service'. (36 68) The 1913 visit to the East was for him a renewal of the sights, smells and sounds of the familiar Islamic world:

> Praised be Allah for the diversity of His creatures and for the Five Advantages of Travel and for the glories of the Cities of the Earth! Harun-al-Raschid, in roaring Bagdad of old, never delighted himself to the limits of such a delight as was mine, that afternoon. . . . And I found myself saying, as perhaps the dead say when they have recovered their wits, *'This is my real world again'.*
>
> (28 273–4. Italics mine.)

The Muslims who appear in his writings give an indication of what attracted him to Islam. Almost all the Muslim characters in Kipling's works are men of action. Gunga Din ('Gunga Din') lays down his life in the discharge of his duties as a water-carrier in the Indian Army. Kamal ('The Ballad of East and West'), the Pathan freebooter, wins the admiration of the Colonel's son for his courage, heroism and sense of honour. The Sudanese Fuzzy-Wuzzy ('Fuzzy-Wuzzy') are worthy fighters. Khoda Dad Khan ('The Head of the District') is portrayed as an honest, strong-willed and brave person. Mahbub Ali (*Kim*), the horse dealer of Lahore, stands for the life of action as opposed to the life of contemplation represented by the Lama. It is thus the Islamic stress on positive action, devotion to duty, discipline and order that seems to have impressed Kipling. On the subject of Islamic emphasis on order, he makes a very explicit statement in *Something of Myself*:

> It is true that the Children of Israel are 'people of the Book', and in the second Surah of the Koran Allah is made to say: 'High above mankind have I raised you.' Yet, later, in the fifth Surah, it is written: 'Oft as they kindle a beacon-fire for war shall God quench it. And their aim will be to abet disorder on the earth; but God loveth not the abettors of disorder.' . . . Israel is a race to leave alone. It abets disorder.
>
> (36 215)

We find therefore that Kipling was deeply aware of Islamic literature and religion, and that he made frequent use of these sources. The practical character of Islamic law also may have helped to define his own realistic approach to moral problems. Though not as pervasive as the Judaeo-Christian tradition, the Islamic tradition has its place in Kipling's intellectual background.

D HINDUISM AND HINDU SOCIETY IN KIPLING'S WORK

Kipling's reaction to Hinduism, generally speaking, was negative. His attitude may partly be explained by the antipathy that a person belonging to a monotheistic school of thought feels towards polytheism. Kipling, who sought unity and design in the universe, was baffled by the intricacies of Hindu mythology and the abstractions of Hindu thought. Moreover it seemed to Kipling that the Hindu attitude towards life was negative or escapist since Hinduism sees the world as *maya* (illusion) — we exist only in the dream of Brahma. It is therefore understandable that Kipling, as an exponent of law, order, discipline and a philosophy of action, reacted strongly against Hinduism.

Thus Kipling often refers to Hindu gods as malignant beings who send only affliction to humanity at large. ' "It is otherwise in Hind," ' says Kim dryly. ' "Their gods are many-armed and malignant. Let them alone." ' (19 83) In the story 'The Bridge-Builders' (1893) we see Shiva the Bull, Ganesha the Elephant, Hanuman the Ape, Kali the Tigress, Bhairon the Buck, Sitala the Ass and Gunga the Crocodile at a *panchayat* (meeting). The gods have assembled to consider the plea of angry Gunga that the Kashi bridge, which is being built over her, be destroyed. In opposing human progress and civilisation, symbolised by bridge-building, the Hindu gods reveal their essential nature. Thus Shiva, the principle of destruction in the *Trimurti* (Hindu Triad), speaks out:

> 'Greater am I than Gunga also. . . . Who smote at Pooree, under the Image there, her thousands in a day and a night, and bound the sickness to the wheels of the fire-carriages, so that it ran from one end of the land to the other? Who but Kali? . . . The fire-carriages have served thee well, Mother of Death. But I speak for mine own altars, who am not Bhairon of the Common folk, but Shiv. Men go to and fro, making words and telling talk of strange Gods, and I listen. Faith follows faith among my people in the schools, and I have no anger; for when the words are said, and the new talk is ended, to Shiv men return at the last.'
>
> (13 40)

Kipling's negative attitude toward Hinduism may further be seen in *The Smith Administration* (1891), a series of sketches of an Anglo-Indian establishment and life in India. For instance 'The Bride's Progress' which originally appeared in *The Pioneer Mail* on 8 February 1888, describes the visit of a newly-married English couple to Benares, the holy city — 'Benares of the Buddhists and the Hindus — of Durga of the Thousand Names — of two Thousand Temples, and twice two thousand stenches.' (16 520) As the couple wander through the narrow streets, 'the symbols of a brutal cult' become apparent:

> Hanuman, red, shameless, and smeared with oil, leaped and leered upon the walls above stolid, black, stone bulls,

knee-deep in yellow flowers. The bells clamoured from
unseen temples, and half-naked men with evil eyes rushed
out of dark places. . . .

(16 521)

After witnessing 'the horrors of a burning *ghat*' (the place
where the Hindu dead are cremated), the couple dive for
the second time into the heart of 'the city of monstrous
creeds':

The walls dripped filth, the pavement sweated filth, and
the contagion of uncleanliness walked among the worshippers. There might have been beauty in the Temple of the
Cow; there certainly was horror enough and to spare; but
The Bride was conscious only of the filth of the place. She
turned to the wisest and best man in the world, asking
indignantly, 'Why don't these horrid people clean the place
out?' 'I don't know,' said The Bridegroom; 'I suppose their
religion forbids it.'

(16 525)

The Bride cannot stand Benares any more, for 'at every
turn lewd gods grinned and mouthed at her, the still air was
clogged with thick odours and the reek of rotten marigold
flowers, and disease stood blind and naked before the sun'.
(16 526) Early the next morning the couple flees from
Benares, and as they catch the last glimpse of the city from
their boat, they hear a *muezzin* defying the Hindu gods:

In the silence a voice thundered far above their heads: '*I
bear witness that there is no God but God.*' It was the
mullah, proclaiming the Oneness of God in the city of the
Million Manifestations. The call rang across the sleeping
city and far over the river, and be sure that the mullah
abated nothing of the defiance of his cry for that he
looked down upon a sea of temples and smelt the incense
of a hundred Hindu shrines.

(16 526–7)

Kipling's dislike of Hinduism was partly based on his deep
awareness of the social evils, and especially the rigid caste
system, of Hindu society. The caste system, it may be noted,
is not simply an economic phenomenon but an integral part

of Hindu religion. In *The Smith Administration,* Kipling sardonically writes about the caste system:

> Those who say that a *mehter* has no caste, speak in ignorance. Those who say that there is a caste in the Empire so mean and so abject that there are no castes below it, speak in greater ignorance. The *arain* says that the *chamar* has no caste; the *chamar* knows that the *mehter* has none; and the *mehter* swears by Lal Beg, his god, that the *od,* whose god is Bhagirat, is without caste. Below the *od* lies the *kaparia-bawaria,* in spite of all that the low-caste *Brahmins* say or do. A *Teji mehter* or a *Sundoo mehter* is as much above a *kaparia-bwaria* as an Englishman is above a *mehter.*
>
> (16 487)

Moreover his father's negative impression of Hindus in general had a great deal to do with Kipling's attitude towards Hinduism. Lockwood Kipling's reaction to Hindus and Hinduism may be gathered from his book *Beast and Man in India: A Popular Sketch of Indian Animals in their Relations With the People* (London, 1891), a source book for the later *Jungle Books.* Here is, for example, a comment on Hindu historians:

> There are many lies in history, but Hindu writers are remarkable for having deliberately and of set principle ignored all the facts of life. All is done, however, with such an air of conviction and pious purpose that we must use Dr Johnson's kindly discrimination and say that they are not inexcusable, but consecrated liars.[13]

And yet, in spite of Kipling's disapproval of Hinduism, Hindu mysticism did have some impact on his mind. This may be seen in the story 'The Miracle of Purun Bhagat' (1894). Here Kipling shows great respect for Sir Purun Dass, a high-caste Brahmin and the Prime Minister of a native state, who becomes a *yogi* (mystic) and meditates in the Himalayas for *ananda* (peace) and *nirvana* (salvation, release from the Wheel). It may, however, be noted that action is still the redeeming feature of the mystic's life in the story. (For a full discussion of this story, see Chapter 5, Section C.)

Kipling was also interested in the Hindu concept of

samsara (continual incarnation). The most striking use of rebirth is in 'The Finest Story in the World' (1891). Here Charlie Mears, a young bank clerk, is able to go back into the past and recollect the happenings of his previous lives as a galley slave and as a ship-mate of one of the Norse explorers of America. Charlie thinks that his memories of the past are just dreams or notions, but the narrator knows that he 'was dealing with the experiences of a thousand years ago, told through the mouth of a boy of today'. (5 128) When the narrator fails to get a full account of the previous cycles of life from Charlie, he turns to the Hindu student Grish Chunder for assistance. Grish Chunder answers in a philosophic vein: ' "*Lekin darwaza band hai.* (Without doubt; but the door is shut.)" ' (5 134)

Kipling, we see, was unsympathetic to the Hindu religion on the whole, yet some specific aspects of Hindu belief appealed to him — and he made use of them in his work.

E BUDDHISM AND THE LAMA IN KIPLING'S WORK

Buddhism, with its middle way, appealed to Kipling greatly. This is amply borne out by *Kim* (1901) which is dominated by the figure of the venerable Teshoo Lama, the abbot of Suchzen monastery in Tibet. The Lama seems at times to be a mouthpiece for Kipling himself. The follower of the 'middle way' projects a vision of brotherhood and love for mankind, none having monopoly over Truth: 'To those who follow the Way there is neither black nor white, Hind nor Bhotiyal. We be all souls seeking escape.' (19 7) It is therefore not surprising that Kipling, who was continuously searching for order and design, was attracted to the synthesizing power of Buddhism.

Kipling evokes the world of Buddhism by reference to some of its famous symbols. The most noted is the *Bhavacakramudra* or 'Wheel of life'. Here is how Kipling describes the Wheel, rich in philosophic symbolism:

He [the Lama] drew from under the table a sheet of strangely scented yellow Chinese paper, the brushes, and the slab of India ink. In cleanest, severest outline he had traced the Great Wheel with its six spokes, whose centre is the conjoined Hog, Snake, and Dove (Ignorance, Anger, and Lust), and whose compartments are all the heavens and hell, and all the chances of human life. Men say that the Bodhisat Himself first drew it with grains of rice upon dust, to teach His disciples the cause of things. Many ages have crystal-lised it into a most wonderful convention crowded with hundreds of little figures whose every line carries a mean-ing.

(19 314—15)

The Buddhist faith is subdivided into two sects, the Hinayana and the Mahayana. The Lama, being a Tibetan, belongs to the Mahayana group to whom two ways are open to gain *nirvana* (salvation): one is *Sutra,* the exoteric way, and the other *Tantra,* the esoteric course. The Lama in *Kim,* as Rao points out, has followed the esoteric course.[14] His search for the River of the Arrow is a 'mystical and magic' way of attaining *nirvana.*

The Eightfold Golden Path of Buddhism is well illustrated by the Lama. The River of the Arrow is only a symbol: it stands for the Lama's desire to reach the Reality behind the *maya* (illusion). With this aim the Lama comes to India where he is helped by the English curator of the Lahore Museum who gives the Lama a map indicating the wanderings of Buddha. With single-mindedness the Lama is going to retrace the steps of Buddha in order to attain enlightenment. Ulti-mately he gives up his physical search for the River of the Arrow; in doing so, the Lama follows the last path of the Eightfold Path: Right Concentration. And now he sees the reality behind the illusion, which leads him to his *nirvana:* 'For the merit that I have acquired, the River of the Arrow is here. It breaks forth at our feet, as I have said.' (19 472)

Thus we see that *Kim* reveals Kipling's deep knowledge and appreciation of the philosophic aspects of Buddhism.

F FREEMASONRY AND KIPLING

On 5 April 1886, being at that time less than twenty-one years of age, Kipling was admitted, under a dispensation from the District Grand Master, to the Order at the Lahore Masonic Lodge, referred to as the *Jadoo-Gher* (Magic House) at the beginning of *Kim*.[15] This is how he describes his initiation in his modest autobiography:

> In '85 I was made a Freemason by dispensation (Lodge Hope and Perseverance 782 E.C.), being under age, because the Lodge hoped for a good Secretary. They did not get him, but I applied, and got the Father to advise, in decorating the bare walls of the Masonic Hall with hangings after the prescription of Solomon's Temple. Here I met Muslims, Hindus, Sikhs, members of the Arya and Brahmo Samaj, and a Jew tyler, who was priest and butcher to his little community in the city. So yet another world opened to me which I needed.
>
> (36 51—2)

On his transfer to Allahabad, he joined Lodge Independence with Philanthropy there. After his departure from India in 1889 Kipling's Masonic activities become difficult to trace. No doubt this was in part due to the author himself, on account of his well-known dislike of personal publicity. But thanks to the labours of Brother Albert Frost, Norfolk Lodge, Sheffield, we can learn a few particulars.[16] It seems fairly certain that he joined the Authors' Lodge in London and, says Brother Frost, he was present at its Consecration in 1910. We are told that 'he was also a member of the Motherland Lodge and a Rosicrucian. . . . He was advanced a Mark Mason in Fidelity Lodge in Lahore and a Royal Ark Mariner of Mount Ararat Lodge attached to the same Lodge. He was an honorary member of Canongate Kilwinning Lodge No. 2, Edinburgh, of which the poet Burns was also an honorary member'.[17]

Freemasonry is an oath-bound fraternal order of men; it draws its name and many of its symbols from the building trade. It admits men of every nationality, religion, colour and political persuasion. It claims to be based upon those fundamentals of religion held in common by all men, and it endeavours to inculcate, through allegories and symbols connected with the art of building, a lofty morality laying particular stress upon benevolence. The essential teachings of Masonry are few and simple, such as belief in a Supreme Being, the brotherhood of man and the desirability of following a moral code.

Kipling's works contain many interesting Masonic allusions, but he is best known to Members of the Craft for two
stories: 'The Man who Would be King' (1888) from *Wee
Willie Winkie* and 'In the Interests of the Brethern' (1918)
included in *Debits and Credits,* and two poems: 'The Mother-
Lodge' (1895) included in *The Seven Seas* and 'Banquet
Night', a foreword to the second of the above-named stories.

'The Man who Would be a King' is a story of two masons,
Brother Peachy Carnehan and Brother Daniel Dravot, who
found a kingdom in Kafiristan on the North West Frontier.
The Masonic note is struck right at the beginning when the
narrator asks one of the brothers in the train: 'Where have
you come from?' And the mason replies: 'From the East and
I am hoping that you will give him the message on the
Square. . . .' In Kafiristan they see the similarity between the
pagan cults of Kafirs and the rituals of Freemasonry, which
helps them in gaining control over the people.

'In the Interests of the Brethern' offers us the clue to
Kipling's attraction to Freemasonry. Men from all walks of
life, whose only practical creed since childhood has been
Masonry — 'The Fatherhood of God, an' the Brotherhood of
Man; an' what more in Hell *do* you want' — find their way to
the Lodge of Instruction, 'Faith and Works 5837', where
they find solace in fellowship and ritual.

'The Mother-Lodge' projects a picture of the cosmopolitan
atmosphere of the Lodge, where the barriers of caste, colour,
and creed break down and men join together in true fellowship:

> We'd Bola Nath, Accountant,
>   An' Saul an Aden Jew,
> An' Din Mohammed, draughtsman
>   Of the Survey Office too;
> There was Babu Chuckerbutty,
>   An' Amir Singh the Sikh,
> An' Castro from the fittin'-sheds,
>   The Roman Catholick! . . .
>
> Full oft on Guv'ment service
>   This rovin' foot 'ath pressed,
> An' bore fraternal greetin's
>   To the Lodges east an' west,

> Accordin' as commanded,
>   From Kohat to Singapore,
> But I wish that I might see them
>   In my Mother-Lodge once more!
>
> I wish that I might see them,
>   My Brethern black an' brown,
> With the trichies smellin' pleasant
>   An' the *hog-darn* passin' down;
> An' the old Khansamah snorin'
>   On the bottle-khana floor,
> Like a Master in good standing
>   With my Mother-Lodge once more.
>   (*DE* 445–6)

Freemasonry confirmed Kipling's faith in the fraternity of mankind as well as in the desirability of following a common moral code. Moreover his practice of Freemasonry reveals his trust in ritual, for ritual after all is an imposition of order that leads to an understanding of a greater order behind the chaos of this material life.

G MITHRAISM IN KIPLING'S WORK

In the Roman stories of *Puck of Pook's Hill* (1906) and in 'The Church that was in Antioch' (1929) Kipling mentions Mithraism. Parnesius and Valens are both followers of Mithras. A Persian god, whose worship spread over the Roman world during the second and third centuries after Christ, Mithras is invoked along with Ormuzd, the sovereign of good, on whose side Mithras always fights. Mithras appears as the god of light, purity, moral goodness and knowledge, engaged in a continual struggle against the power of evil. Victory in this battle can be attained only by sacrifice and probation, and Mithras is perceived as always performing the mystic sacrifice through which the good will triumph.

The Mithraic faith, personal in character and applying the processes of the struggles and regeneration of nature to the case of the human soul, had in it much to satisfy real moral needs. Throughout stress is laid on the constant struggle between good and evil. The defeat of evil calls for moral rectitude. Given that rectitude, however, victory is assured both in this world and in the world to come, since Mithras the unconquered is ever on the side of the faithful.

Mithraism provided Kipling with proof of similarities between diverse religious traditions. He was delighted to find analogies between Mithraism and Masonry. Though religious scholars believe that the similarities between Christianity and Mithraism (belief in a divine Lord by whose deeds man is assured of salvation, belief in a sacramental meal, a ritual of baptism, a moral code, and so forth) have their roots in a common Eastern origin rather than in any borrowing by the one from the other, it is entirely in keeping with Kipling's philosophy that Valens should say to his uncle ' "that there isn't a ceremony or symbol that they [the Christians] haven't stolen from the Mithra ritual" '. (33 97) Similarly, the analogy between Mithraism and Masonry is underlined when in the Puck stories Parnesius says that he and Pertinax were raised to the ' "Degree of Gryphons" ' together.

The philosophy of action advocated by Mithraism was in keeping with Kipling's line of thinking. Kipling must have been pleased to discover that Mithraism was particularly popular in the Roman armies, and that a soldier of Mithras had to be upright and morally pure: as Lucius Sergius, the head of the Antioch urban police, says to his nephew, ' "It's a soldier's religion, even though it does come from outside." ' (33 97)

H SUMMARY

We have seen that although Kipling was brought up as a Christian, he did not conform to that or to any of the other major orthodox religions of the world, as he was attracted by their essential spirit rather than by their external forms. In the Judaeo-Christian tradition, the biblical law and the values of sacrifice, suffering and love influenced him greatly. Similarly the Islamic emphasis on positive action, law and order seems to have impressed him. His reaction towards Hinduism was negative, for it appeared to him that the Hindu attitude towards life was escapist and its social structure too rigid; but Buddhism, a reformed version of Hinduism, appealed to him. Freemasonry confirmed his faith in a universal moral order as well as the brotherhood of mankind. And he likewise admired Mithraism for its emphasis on moral conduct, making it a touchstone for some of his own particular views. It is clear therefore, even from a brief survey such as this, that diverse and divergent religious traditions entered into the shaping of Kipling's moral and ethical views, helping to solidify his conception of Law.

4 The Imperial Order

Mary, Mother av Mercy, fwat the devil possist us to take an'
kape this melancholious counthry? Answer me that, sorr.
Private Mulvaney in 'With the Main Guard', 2 150

A HISTORICAL BACKGROUND

The root idea of empire in the ancient and medieval world
was that of a federation of states, under a universal law and a
hegemony, covering the entire known world, such as was held
by Rome under the so-called *pax Romana*. This conception
of a single empire wielding authority over the world did not
disappear with the fall of Rome — it survived all the fluctua-
tions of the Holy Roman Empire. And in later ages this
dream of a universal empire animated the policies of Peter
the Great, Catherine and Napoleon. The idea of a universal
empire was not confined to the West alone — witness the
Chinese and Byzantine empires; and political philosophers in
many ages — Confucius, Dante, Machiavelli, Vico, Kant —
have speculated on the concept.

A universal empire, though founded by conquests and
bloodshed, is based on a philosophy of peace, secure order,
discipline and internationalism. Seen in these terms, the universal empire becomes an antithesis of disorder, chaos and
anarchy, and satisfies the deep-seated human desire for unity
rather than division. With this mission the universal empire
raises a vision of utopia justifying power as well as the possibility of a solution for the woes of mankind.

This positive Imperial Idea fascinated Kipling, and it forms
one of the most important factors in the shaping of Kipling's
mind, art and vision. Kipling has, however, been equated with
the rather vague term 'imperialism', and he has been seen as a
prophet of the British Empire: these are gross over-
simplifications of his complex attitude toward the Imperial
Idea. As we shall see, Kipling's ideal was based on the philosophic concept of empire as a positive force that imposes a

pattern of order on chaos, and he admired the British Empire in which he perceived certain manifestations of the true Imperial Idea. Kipling sang of those positive aspects. Yet he was not the only one to notice the positive principle behind certain facets of the Empire; theories of an imperial ideal were very much in the air at the end of the nineteenth century. At this stage it will be useful to go through some aspects of the British Imperialism of the late nineteenth and early twentieth centuries to understand the imperial philosophy of Kipling.

Generally speaking it was during the last quarter of the nineteenth century that a new mood of imperialism became prevalent in England. Historians have shown in detail how much of this new disposition was activated by reaction against the separatist tendencies which had been very strong during the middle of the nineteenth century. About 1830 a small but vocal group of Radicals and Whigs calling themselves Colonial Reformers made its appearance on the British scene. The Colonial Reformers may be regarded as the forerunners of modern imperialism. Their main aim was the preservation of the unity of the Empire. They contributed two important ideas to the colonial policy of the time: systematic colonization and responsible self-government. The Colonial Reformers were, however, soon challenged by a different school of thought, the Manchester School, which became a strong force in the seventies. The leading figures of the Manchester School were Cobden and Bright with Professor Goldwin Smith as its literary exponent. The main tenets of this group were a *laissez-faire* economic policy, a thorough revision of the financial side of colonial relationships with Britain, a disregard for sentimental ties with overseas dependent colonies, and a strong anti-military conviction. Goldwin Smith even advocated that Britain should rid herself of the colonies.

The climax of the separatist influence occurred around 1870 and then, with curious suddenness, came the beginnings of that utterly different school of thought we call imperialism. In 1868 a number of private individuals formed a non-political body, the Royal Colonial Institute, 'for the purpose of promoting in England a better knowledge of the

colonies and of India'.[1] The group was later termed 'The
Colonial Society', and its motto was 'United Empire'. From
1870 onwards a stream of articles appeared in contemporary
magazines, especially *Fraser's Magazine,* in which a new note
is discernible — J. A. Froude attacks the government for its
alleged lack of interest in the colonies and Edward Jenkins
protests against the dissolution of 'this marvellous empire'.[2]
The beginning of 1871 saw the emergence of the concept of
imperial federation. The Federationists, recommending the
adoption of an imperial constitution with an imperial parlia-
ment and an imperial cabinet for imperial affairs, were
popularly welcomed with a favourable climate of opinion.

In 1872 Benjamin Disraeli, then leader of the opposition,
committed the Conservative party to the imperial cause in his
famous Crystal Palace speech. He angrily attacked the Liberal
party for its part in the disintegration of the Empire and his
speech ended with an exhortation which, forgetting the
colonies, concentrated on the emotional aspect of the name
Empire:

> The issue is not a mean one. It is whether you will be
> content to be a comfortable England, modelled and
> moulded upon Continental principles and meeting in due
> course an inevitable fate, or whether you will be a great
> country, an Imperial country, a country where your sons,
> when they rise, rise to paramount positions, and obtain
> not merely the esteem of their countrymen but command
> the respect of the world.[3]

'That,' says Buckle, Disraeli's biographer, 'is the famous
declaration from which the modern conception of the British
Empire largely takes its rise.'[4]

In 1874 when Disraeli and the Conservatives came into
power, his policies strove towards his stated goal of two years
before, namely the possession of an empire on which the sun
never set. Awareness of the Empire and especially of the
Indian Empire was growing and under the Royal Titles Act of
1876 the Queen assumed the title of Empress of India.

Meanwhile the literature of imperialism appeared. In 1883
John Robert Seeley, a professor of history at Cambridge,
emerged as one of the most prominent exponents of im-

perialism with the publication of his book *The Expansion of England.* Seeley, like Froude, maintained that the colonies offered the key to Britain's history, suggesting moral rather than mercenary arguments for imperialism.

By the eighties Empire had become the symbol of two aspirations: a desire to strengthen the bonds between the colonies and the mother country, and a belief in the providential destiny of the English race to bring civilization to Asia and Africa. The imperial mood then prevalent was given royal sanction in the Queen's Speech at the end of the parliamentary session in September 1886: ' "There is on all sides a growing desire to draw closer in every practical way the bonds which unite the various portions of the Empire." '[5] To be called an 'imperialist' in 1886 was a compliment, not abuse.[6]

The missionary zeal or the so-called 'White Man's Burden' played a very important role from the beginning in this change of attitude towards imperialism. According to Hakluyt's *Voyages* Edward Hay, who accompanied Sir H. Gilbert on his voyage to the New World in 1583, thought that 'the discoverie and planting' of remote countries could only succeed if their chief aim was the sowing of Christianity. Later missionaries worked — in the spirit of Livingstone — to bring honest trade and the Word of God to 'heathen' peoples. Their influence was most marked in the earlier part of the nineteenth century, when there was a stronger proselytizing element in British Imperialism than at any other time.

Towards the later half of the nineteenth century, however, the emphasis shifted from an effort to convert people to Christianity to a greater concern for the eradication of social evils, education, better means of communication and other works of public welfare. This change in missionary emphasis is related to changes in Christian thinking: there was a growing lack of certainty about some basic religious matters, and there was also the emergence of a new theology called the 'social gospel'. One can cite F. D. Maurice and his Christian socialism.

It was the 'White Man's Burden' which appealed to Kipling and the new British imperialists. Chamberlain, speaking at a Royal Colonial Institute dinner in 1897, regretted the bloodshed involved in imperial conquests, in bringing ' "these countries into some kind of disciplined order," ' but, he added, ' "it must be remembered that that is the condition of the mission we have to fulfil" '.[7] Milner, for example, believed the *Pax Britannica* to be ' "essential to the maintenance of civilized conditions of existence among one-fifth of the human race" ' who lacked ' "the gift of maintaining peace and order for themselves" '.[8]

It should be borne in mind that the evolutionary philosophy current at the time lay at the back of the missionary motives. Perhaps Froude gave the most complete expression to these sentiments:

> We have another function such as the Romans had. The sections of men on this globe are unequally gifted. Some are strong and can govern themselves; some are weak and are the prey of foreign invaders and internal anarchy; and freedom which all desire, is only attainable by weak nations when they are subject to the rule of others who are at once powerful and just. This was the duty which fell to the Latin race two thousand years ago. In these modern times it has fallen to ours, and in the discharge of it the highest features in the English character have displayed themselves.[9]

The writers and public figures of the period can be cited to show how widespread the imperial mood was in the eighties and the nineties:

> To the English People in World History . . . There have been, shall I prophesy, two grand tasks assigned: Huge-looming through the tumult of the always incommensurable Present Time, outlines of the two tasks disclose themselves: the grand industrial task of conquering some half or more of this terraqueous planet for the use of man; then secondly, the grand Constitutional task of sharing in some pacific endurable manner, the fruit of said conquest, and showing how it might be done. (Carlyle, *Chartism*)[10]

> There is a destiny now possible to us, the highest ever set before a nation to be accepted or refused. We are still

undegenerate in race; a race mingled of the best northern blood. . . . This is what England must either do, or perish; she must found colonies as fast and as far as she is able, formed of her most energetic and worthiest men; . . . their first aim is to be to advance the power of England by land and sea. . . .(Ruskin, Inaugural Lecture at Oxford, 1870)[11]

But let it be our ideal all the same. To fight for the right, to abhor the imperfect, the unjust, or the mean, to swerve neither to the right hand not to the left, to care nothing for flattery or applause or odium or abuse — it is so easy to have any of them in India — never to let your enthusiasm be soured or your courage grow dim, but to remember that the Almighty has placed your hand on the greatest of His ploughs, in whose furrow the nations of the future are germinating and taking shape, to drive the blade a little forward in your time, and to feel that somewhere among these millions you have left a little justice or happiness or prosperity, . . . a dawn of intellectual enlightenment, or a stirring of duty, where it did not before exist — that is enough, that is the Englishman's justification in India. (Lord Curzon, Speech in Bombay, 16 November 1905)[12]

We happen to be the best people in the world, with the highest ideals of decency and justice and liberty and peace, and the more of the world we inhabit, the better it is for humanity. (Cecil Rhodes)[13]

These quotations give us a feeling for the imperially charged atmosphere of the times. Even Gladstone had to admit that the sentiment of empire ' "may be called innate in every Briton. If there are exceptions, they are like those men born blind or lame among us. It is part of our patrimony: born with our birth, dying with our death. . . ." '[14] The Empire was a living reality, but the imperialism of the late Victorian period went deeper than any political action or theory: it was a subjective feeling beyond deliberate policy, and its foundations, at least from the British point of view, were humanitarian and moral rather than exclusively mercenary. At this stage imperialism had become, as Cecil

Rhodes put it, a philosophy of 'philanthropy plus five per cent'.[15]

Kipling has too often been condemned for being an imperialist, but put in the context of his times I do not see how one can expect a writer, endowed with a most sensitive eye and ear, to be blind and deaf to the ideas current at his particular moment in history. Furthermore it was perfectly natural that Kipling should have felt the impact of the Empire and the Imperial Idea more tangibly than other writers in England, as he himself explains: 'And what should they know of England who only England know?' (11 143) Kipling proudly acknowledges that the Imperial Idea was central to his work. In a well-known passage in his autobiography, *Something of Myself* (1937), he says:

> Bit by bit my original notion grew into a vast, vague, conspectus — Army and Navy Stores List if you like — of the whole sweep and meaning of things and efforts and origins throughout the Empire. I visualised it, as I do most ideas, in the shape of a semi-circle of buildings and temples projecting into a sea of dreams.

(36 87—8)

At another place in his autobiography he speaks of the Sussex stories as 'a sort of balance to, as well as a seal upon, some aspects of my "Imperialistic" output in the past'. (36 182)

However Kipling's imperialism, as it will be shown in the following pages, cannot be identified with British imperialism alone. It is a much larger concept that can be traced more generally to the idea of a universal empire based on principles of law, order, service and sacrifice.

B A CASE FOR KIPLING

Despite Kipling's statement that the Imperialist message was central to his work, to read him solely in terms of politics or history or journalistic reportage is hardly just. Such an approach would be very superficial indeed, and it would not take us beyond the surface meaning of Kipling's work. No one, of course, can deny the intimate relationship between Imperialism and Kipling, and there are as a matter of fact

some stories of obvious political and propagandist nature —
'The Enlightenments of Pagett, M.P.' (1890) and 'The Head
of the District' (1890) are ready examples. However stories
of this type are very few, and to read these stories merely in
terms of the surface pattern is to lose sight of what Noel
Annan has termed 'the riddle of Kipling'.

For instance 'The Enlightenments of Pagett, M.P.' is not
simply a vigorous defence of Anglo-Indian domination of
India: it is also a part of Kipling's study of social realities. In
this story Pagett, a Liberal M.P., comes to India on a fact-
finding mission to assess the extent of Indian aspirations for
independence. Orde, the Deputy-Commissioner of Amara and
an old friend of Pagett, shows him around and tries to con-
vince him that the average Indian has not even heard about
the Congress and that the English rule is in fact beneficial for
India. At Orde's office Pagett meets a cross section of Indian
society, and all of them, with the sole exception of the young
Indian student Dinanath, express indifference to or ignorance
of the Indian National Congress. While there is some exag-
geration and forcing of points here and there, one must con-
cede that there is a great deal of truth in what Kipling is
saying in this story.

The first real Indian whom Pagett meets at Orde's office is
a Punjabi Sikh, Bishen Singh, a carpenter by profession. The
picture of the Sikh appears to be authentic:

> He began with laboured respect to explain how he was a
> poor man with no concern in such matters, which were all
> under the control of God, but presently broke out of Urdu
> into familiar Punjabi, the mere sound of which had a rustic
> smack of village smoke-reek and plough-tail, as he de-
> nounced the wearers of white coats, the jugglers with
> words who filched his field from him, the men whose
> backs were never bowed in honest work; and poured ironi-
> cal scorn on the Bengali.
>
> (4 352–3)

Bishen Singh's story of the oppression and exploitation of
petty farmers and artisans by 'men whose backs were never
bowed in honest work' can be corroborated by the 'raw and
naked humanity' of the subcontinent. The Sikh's hatred of

the Bengali prompts Orde's remark: 'Pride of race, which also means race-hatred, is the plague and curse of India and it spreads far.' Orde goes on to elaborate his statement:

'There's the Afghan, and, as a highlander, he despises all the dwellers in Hindustan — with the exception of the Sikh, whom he hates as cordially as the Sikh hates him. The Hindu loathes Sikh and Afghan, and the Rajput — that's a little lower down across this yellow blot of desert — has a strong objection, to put it mildly, to the Maratha, who, by the way, poisonously hates the Afghan. Let's go North a minute. The Sindhi hates everybody I've mentioned. Very good, we'll take less warlike races. The cultivator of Northern India domineers over the man in the next province, and the Behari of the North-West ridicules the Bengali.'

(4 354)

Anyone who knows the subcontinent will agree with Orde that racial prejudice was and is still the root trouble in India.

Kipling's references to the opposition to the Congress by many Indian groups are not spurious either. The Indian Muslims, generally speaking, were suspicious of the Hindu-dominated Congress and ultimately they parted ways, forming the Muslim League which led to the formation of Pakistan. Thus Rasul Ali Khan, the old Muslim landed gentleman who impresses Pagett with his 'distinction of manner and fine appearance', expresses genuine scorn for the Congress, as Orde explains:

'When you are sure of a majority, election is a fine system; but you can scarcely expect the Mahommedans, the most masterful and powerful minority in the country, to contemplate their own extinction with joy. . . . They say little, but after all they are the most important faggots in the great bundle of communities, and all the glib bunkum in the world would not pay for their estrangement. They have controlled the land.'

(4 357–8)

Orde's explanation is perfectly true, and it gives the common Muslim point of view *vis-à-vis* the Congress. Later in the story even Dinanath has to admit that Muslims and Christians are not enthusiastic about the Congress.

Next comes old Jelloo, the Jat farmer, who is drawn with great realism and sensitivity:

> His strongly marked features glowed with russet bronze, and his bright eyes gleamed under deeply set brows, contracted by lifelong exposure to sunshine. His beard and moustache, streaked with gray, swept from bold cliffs of brow and cheek in the large sweeps one sees drawn by Michael Angelo, and strands of long black hair mingled with the irregularly piled wreaths and folds of his turban. The drapery of stout blue cotton cloth thrown over his broad shoulders and girt round his narrow loins, hung from his tall form in broadly sculptured folds and he would have made a superb model for an artist in search of a patriarch.
>
> (4 362)

The farmer's sentiments about the native police are also not incredible, for the corruption of Indian police is an open secret: ' "the police were rather worse than small-pox and criminal tribes put together," ' Jelloo remarks. As far as the Congress is concerned, Jelloo has never heard of it; this is quite probable, for the Indian farmer was worried about keeping body and soul together and less concerned about lofty idealism. In an early poem Kipling presents a realistic picture of the Indian farmer:

> And the Ploughman settled the share
> More deep in the sun-dried clod: —
> 'Mogul, Mahratta, and *Mlech* from the North,
> And White Queen over the Seas —
> God raiseth them up and driveth them forth
> As the dust of the ploughshare flies in the breeze;
> But the wheat and the cattle are all my care,
> And the rest is the will of God.'
>
> ('What The People Said' (1887), *DE* 67)

Stories like 'The Englightenment of Pagett, M.P.' should be viewed in the context of Kipling's thought. From this perspective the remarks of Edwards, an old friend of Pagett, become significant: 'There are no politics, in a manner of

speaking, in India. It's all work.' (4 350) Edwards' statement
is confirmed by the passionate rhetoric of the American doctor, Eva McCreery Lathrop, chief of the new Women's
Hospital in Amara:

> 'Well, what's the matter with this country is not in the
> least political, but an all-round entanglement of physical,
> social, and moral evils and corruptions, all more or less due
> to the unnatural treatment of women. You can't gather
> figs from thistles, and so long as the system of infant
> marriage, the prohibition of remarriage of widows, the life-
> long imprisonment of wives and mothers in a worse than
> penal confinement, and the witholding from them any
> kind of education or treatment as rational beings con-
> tinues, the country can't advance a step. Half of it is
> morally dead, and worse than dead, and that's just the half
> from which we have a right to look for the best impulses.
> It's right here where the trouble is, and not in any political
> considerations whatsoever.'

(4 380)

Dr Lathrop's statement may not be entirely accurate, but
there is a great deal of truth in it if it is seen in the context of
its time, the end of the nineteenth century. But what is important is that such statements show the way in which
Kipling's mind works. One can see that Kipling's attitude is
thoroughly pragmatic: all around him he saw India's mass of
'raw, brown, naked humanity' more in need of basic facilities
than abstract democratic theories.

Similarly critics have strongly objected to another story
'The Head of the District' on the grounds that it presents the
thesis that Indians are incapable of governing themselves.
This may be true in so far as Kipling did believe that Indians
could not stand on their own feet at least at that point in
history, but I do not think that this is the precise thesis of
the story. The story is about a very capable Bengali Hindu
Grish Chunder De, M.A., who is 'more English than the
English'. He was a member of the Bengal Civil Service and
was quite a successful administrator: 'He was cultured, of the
world, and, if report spoke truly, had wisely and, above all,
sympathetically ruled a crowded district in South-Eastern
Bengal.' (4 175)

It is, however, when Grish Chunder is transferred on Orde's death to the turbulent North West Frontier Province that the trouble starts. The reason offered by Kipling is that the warlike Muslim Pathans who inhabit the North West Frontier bordering Afghanistan refuse to submit to a Bengali Hindu Babu; this is very convincing. Khoda Dad Khan questions Tallantire, Orde's assistant: ' "But, O Sahib, has the Government gone mad to send a black Bengali dog to us? And am I to pay service to such a one? And are you to work under him? What does it mean?" ' And he goes on to explain: ' "All the people of the earth have harried Bengal. It is written. Thou knowest when we of the North wanted women or plunder whither went we? To Bengal — where else?" ' (4 184)

The thesis of this story is not that an Indian cannot be a good administrator, for Grish Chunder De is certainly a successful and capable civil servant; the point of the story, which ends in the murder of Grish Chunder's brother and his own flight, is that Muslims cannot tolerate Hindus as their masters even though they may be well qualified for the job. This is a valid observation indeed, for Muslims had ruled India for almost one thousand years, and though the Moghul Empire was lost to the British the haughty Muslims still could not reconcile themselves to Hindu domination.

This story indirectly points to another related fact. Hindus and especially Bengali Hindus led India in education and therefore they acquired most of the positions reserved for Indians in the Civil Service. This was naturally resented by Muslims. Sir Sayyid, one of the most prominent Muslim leaders of the subcontinent and a member of the Viceroy's Council, strongly opposed the demands of the Congress for recruitment of Indians in the Civil Service through competitive examinations:

> He [Sir Sayyid] maintained that, in the conditions then existing in India, compliance with the demands made by the Congress would injure the state. Competitive examinations, though suitable in English conditions, would in India lead to the selection of officials whose origin would make them unacceptable to the strongly conservative Indian with his pride in ancestry. . . . The Bengalis, who were

likely to gain most of the posts, would not be submitted to by Muslims and Rajputs with their warlike traditions.[16]

Most probably this speech by Sir Sayyid, delivered in 1887, gave Kipling the material for 'The Head of the District' (1890). Here Kipling, in the light of his own experiences, confirms Sir Sayyid's position that university degrees alone are not sufficient to justify the appointment of bookish Bengali Babus as administrators of the warlike Muslims of the North West Frontier.

Thus we see that 'The Enlightenments of Pagett, M.P.' and 'The Head of the District' cannot be dismissed as sheer propaganda — they are based on hard, real facts of life in India — but stories of this type are very few.

One must keep in mind that Kipling is basically an artist and that he is not a political philosopher in the strict sense of the term. As an imaginative artist he has every right to present his own view or version of things, with which one may or may not agree. The point is that one cannot expect a dispassionate, balanced, consistent and comprehensive view of society from an artist. One must distinguish between the truth of fact and the truth of imagination.

C INDIA: KIPLING'S VISION OF CHAOS

The central character of Kipling's Indian writings is the 'great, grey, formless India' which, like Nature in Hardy's novels, remains the permanent, relentless, malignant and indefinable Being that broods over this little world of ours. India attracts and repels Kipling simultaneously. On the one hand the tender childhood bond between Kipling and this mysterious Being, India — the land of 'light and colour and golden and purple fruit' — draws him irresistibly toward her; and on the other hand the mature Kipling, preoccupied with ideas of order and discipline, is baffled by this strange land where he cannot discover any well-defined pattern. Through Kim Kipling confesses that his attitude towards India is ambivalent:

> Something I owe to the soil that grew —
> More to the life that fed —

But most to Allah Who gave me two
Separate sides to my head.
(19 214)

Although it is particularly in *Kim* (1901) that Kipling's
love for India comes to the fore, on the whole India remains
the 'great Sphinx of the Plains' (4 305) whose riddle of
ambivalence cannot be solved. India overwhelms and crushes
one in every respect. Speaking to Mrs Hauksbee in 'The
Education of Otis Yeere' (1888), Mrs Mallow remarks:
'Surely twelve Simla seasons ought to have taught you that
you can't focus anything in India. . . . We are only little bits
of dirt on the hillsides — here one day and blown down the
khud [hillside] the next.' (6 9—10) There is a strange lack of
atmosphere in India that contributes to the blurring of
vision:

One of the many curses of our life in India is the want of
atmosphere in the painter's sense. There are no half-tints
worth noticing. Men stand out all crude and raw, with
nothing to tone them down, and nothing to scale them
against.

(1 322)

Kipling's symbol for this lack of clarity in India is the
duststorm, used effectively in 'False Dawn' (1888). This
story tells how Saumarez gives a moonlight riding party at an
old tomb beside the bed of a river in an out-of-the-way sta-
tion in order to propose to the elder Miss Copleigh. Everything is fine until supper is ready, and then suddenly:

. . . the moon went out and a burning hot wind began
lashing the orange-trees with a sound like the noise of the
sea. Before we knew where we were, the dust-storm was on
us and everything was roaring whirling darkness. . . . It was
a grand storm. The wind seemed to be pitching it to lee-
ward in great heaps; and the heat beat up from the ground
like the heat of the Day of Judgement.

(1 60—1)

In the topsy-turvy created by the storm Saumarez proposes
to the wrong girl; the mistake is rectified only when the

storm abates. The duststorm is a symbol of India's confusion.
Kipling also finds India's 'want of atmosphere' in its absolutes of light and darkness. India's brightness is dazzling —
the blazing sun, ironically enough, becomes an instrument of
blindness rather than light. India goes dead by day, and she
comes to life only in darkness. Thus one can understand
Kipling's preoccupation with night, dark *gullies* (streets) in
the walled areas of an Indian city, dark *divans* (halls) of old
castles, *chandoo-khanas* (opium houses) in a gully near the
Mosque of Wazir Khan in Lahore, ghosts and grave-yards.
After his office hours young Kipling loved to roam around
the walled city of Lahore at night:

> Often the night got into my head as it had done in the
> boarding-house in the Brompton Road, and I would wan-
> der till dawn in all manner of odd places — liquor shops,
> gambling and opium dens, which are not a bit mysterious,
> wayside entertainments such as puppet-shows, native
> dances; or in and out about the narrow gullies under the
> Mosque of Wazir Khan for the sheer sake of looking. . . .
> One would come home, just as the light broke, in some
> night-hawk of a hired carriage which stank of hookah
> fumes, jasmine-flowers, and sandalwood; and if the driver
> were moved to talk, he told one a good deal. *Much of real
> Indian life goes on in the hot weather nights.*
>
> (36 52—3. Italics mine.)

Despite his frequent night prowls Kipling's India remains
inscrutable:

> You'll never plumb the Oriental mind,
> And if you did it isn't worth the toil.
> Think of a sleek French priest in Canada;
> Divide by twenty half-breeds. Multiply
> By twice the Sphinx's silence. There's your East,
> And you're as wise as ever.
>
> ('One Viceroy Resigns' (1888), *DE* 69—70)

India also manifests herself as evil and cruel, a malignant or
negative force in Kipling's works. First and foremost of the
negative traits is the adverse and hostile Indian climate which,
in Kipling's hands, becomes a sinister force destroying all

aliens and making India the 'grim step-mother' and 'the land of regrets'. Private Simmons's tragedy in the story 'In the Matter of a Private' (1888) and Dicky Hatt's motive for committing suicide in 'In the Pride of his Youth' (1887) are largely due to the intense heat of India. 'The City of Dreadful Night' (1885) gives a 'feel' for the 'dense wet heat' which hangs over Lahore:

> The dense wet heat that hung over the face of land, like a blanket, prevented all hope of sleep in the first instance. The cicalas helped the heat; and the yelling jackals the cicalas. It was impossible to sit still in the dark, empty, echoing house and watch the punkah beat the dead air.
>
> (4 35)

It is especially in the outposts of India that the Indian weather can be seen at its most active in its relentless war against the aliens. 'At the End of the Passage' (1890) is about four lonely Anglo-Indians who are stationed in isolated places in the Indian Empire away from home and civilization. Mottram of the Indian Survey, Lowndes of the Civil Service and Spurstow of the Medical Department get together at Hummil's house to relax for a few hours. Yet cruel India cannot tolerate any aliens — it has already killed Hummil's assistant and now it is Hummil's turn:

> The atmosphere within was only 104°, as the thermometer bore witness, and heavy with the foul smell of badly-trimmed kerosene lamps; and this stench, combined with that of native tobacco, baked brick, and dried earth, sends the heart of many a strong man down to his boots, for it is the smell of the Great Indian Empire when she turns herself for six months into a house of torment. . . . The night-light was trimmed; the shadow of the punkah wavered across the room, and the *'flick'* of the punkah-towel and the soft whine of the rope through the wall-hole followed it. Then the punkah flagged, almost ceased. The sweat poured from Spurstow's brow. Should he go out and harangue the coolie? It started forward again with a savage jerk, and a pin came out of the towels. When this was replaced, a tomtom in the coolie-lines began to beat with

the steady throb of a swollen artery inside some brain-fevered skull.

(5 345)

And Hummil does die of heat-apoplexy in the end.

Death, decay and disease going hand in hand with heat in India are further signs of her malignancy. In *Something of Myself* (1937) Kipling writes:

> Death was always our near companion. . . . The dead of all times were about us — in the vast forgotten Muslim cemeteries round the Station, where one's horse's hoof of a morning might break through to the corpse below; skulls and bones tumbled out of our mud garden walls, and were turned up among the flowers by the Rains; and at every point were tombs of the dead.
>
> (36 41–2)

This is what Orde tells Pagett in 'The Enlightenments of Pagett, M.P.': ' "We work on the refuse of worked-out cities and exhausted civilizations, among the bones of the dead." ' (4 385)

One is always conscious of the presence of death in Kipling's Indian stories. It claims the only son of poor Imam Din, it makes Lispeth an orphan by killing her parents through cholera, it snatches away little Tota — that bond of love between Holden and Ameera — through seasonal fever, it takes away five children of McKenna at Jhansi, it takes the form of a furious revenge in 'Dray Wara Yow Dee' (1888), and it lays waste entire villages and towns in one stroke. While reading these tales one can imagine that familiar Western medieval figure — black-robed Death — fast at work in India:

> India . . . is not a golden country, though poets have sung otherwise. There men die with great swiftness, and those who live suffer many and curious things.
>
> ('The Incarnation of Krishna Mulvaney' (1889), 2 42)

These words sound like a Greek chorus lamenting the fate of man. In his autobiography, Kipling comments:

> Heaven knows the men died fast enough from typhoid,

which seemed to have something to do with water, but we were not sure; or from cholera, which was manifestly a breath of the Devil that could kill all on one side of a barrack-room and spare the others; from seasonal fever; or from what was described as 'blood-poisoning'.

(36 55)

It is not surprising then that people in the Club take a regular stock of their losses:

Everybody was there and there was a general closing up of ranks and taking stock of our losses in dead or disabled that had fallen during the past year. It was a very wet night, and I remember that we sang 'Auld Lang Syne' with our feet in the Polo Championship Cup and our heads among the stars, and swore that we were all very dear friends.

('The Mark of the Beast' (1890), 5 171)

And here is a picture of a famine striking South India:

Here the people crawled to the side of the train, holding their little ones in their arms; and a loaded truck would be left behind, men and women clustering round and above it like ants by spilled honey. Once in the twilight they saw on a dusty plain a regiment of little brown men, each bearing a body over his shoulder; and when the train stopped to leave yet another truck, they perceived that the burdens were not corpses, but only foodless folk picked up beside their dead oxen by a corps of Irregular troops.

('William the Conqueror' (1895), 13 238)

The negative character of India is further revealed in Kipling's depiction of rampant chaos and confusion. For Kipling India is a cruel deity who promotes disharmony among the people who are doomed to live under her sway. This disorder usually takes the form of religious and linguistic riots — a ritual which the people in India have to go through periodically. Mention has already been made of Orde's perceptive comment that racial and religious prejudice are the curse of India, and this is fully illustrated in the story 'On the City Wall' (1888).

'On the City Wall' is set in the house of Lalun, a dancing girl of Lahore, where men of all faiths and all walks of life come to hear her songs on the *sitar*. Wali Dad, a young educated Muslim and the chief admirer of Lalun, tells the narrator: ' "Outside of a Freemason's Lodge I have never seen such gatherings." ' However this little scene of mirth, gaiety and fellowship is not tolerated by the gods of India who only enjoy sending affliction to humanity at large. So this happy picture of harmony is set within a contrasting framework. The city of Lahore is engulfed in a tense communal atmosphere for Muharram, the great mourning-festival of Muslims (properly the Shi'ah), is close at hand. All day the Muharram drums beat in the City, and deputations of tearful Hindus besiege the Deputy Commissioner for assurance of their safety. ' "Which," said the Deputy Commissioner in confidence to the Head of Police, "is a pretty fair indication that the Hindus are going to make 'emselves unpleasant." ' (4 324)

It is on the night of the Muharram procession that the above-mentioned picture of harmony within the four walls of Lalun's house is painted. Suddenly the cries of *'Ya Hasan, Ya Hussain'* fill the air and the people look down from the window of Lalun's room:

> The drums were beating fresh, the crowd were howling *'Ya Hasan! Ya Hussain!'* and beating their breasts, the brass bands were playing their loudest, and at every corner where space allowed, Muhammedan preachers were telling the lamentable story of the death of the Martyrs. . . . As the first *tazia,* a gorgeous erection ten feet high, was borne aloft on the shoulders of a score of stout men into the semi-darkness of the Gully of the Horsemen, a brickbat crashed through its talc and tinsel sides.
>
> (4 326)

This is the start of the trouble, and soon there is general fighting:

> The *tazias* rocked like ships at sea, the long pole-torches dipped and rose round them, while the men shouted: 'The Hindus are dishonouring the *tazias!* Strike! Strike! Into their temples for the Faith!' The six or eight Policemen

with each *tazia* drew their batons, and struck as long as
they could in the hope of forcing the mob forward, but
they were overpowered, and as contingents of Hindus
poured into the streets the fight became general.

(4 327)

One gets another glimpse of communal riots in 'His Chance
in Life' (1887):

Tibasu was a forgotten little place with a few Orissa
Mohammedans in it. These, hearing nothing of the Collec-
tor-*Sahib* for some time and heartily despising the Hindu
Sub-Judge, arranged to start a little Moharrum riot of their
own. But the Hindus turned out and broke their heads;
when, finding lawlessness pleasant, Hindus and Mohammedans together raised an aimless sort of Donnybrook just
to see how far they could go. They looted each other's shops,
and paid off private grudges in the regular way.

(1 88–9)

In 'Namgay Doola' (1891) a cow's tail is cut off, setting
the mood for violence:

Next morning the Kingdom was in uproar. Namgay Doola,
men said, had gone forth in the night and with a sharp
knife hat cut off the tail of a cow belonging to the rabbit-
faced villager who had betrayed him. It was sacrilege un-
speakable against the Holy Cow. The State desired his
blood, but he had retreated into his hut, barricaded the
doors and windows with big stones, and defied the world.

(4 28)

This lawlessness, prompted by the cruel goddess India,
takes many shapes. Besides riots, one of the forms in which
these forces of disorder manifest themselves is devotion to
the primitive code of honour and revenge, which modern
civilised man fails to understand. In 'Dray Wara Yow Dee'
(1888), written as a Browningesque dramatic monologue, we
see this primitive force in the insatiable thirst for vengeance of
a fierce Pathan who is pursuing his wife's lover through deserts, isolated hamlets, flooded rivers and humming cities. He
does not care for the modern law; he is following his own
code sactioned by the spirit of India that has already allowed

him to mutilate his wife's body. And the elderly Pathan frankly
expresses his attitude to the Englishman's law:

> Your Law! What is your Law to me? When the horses fight
> on the runs do they regard the boundary pillars; or do the
> kites of Ali Musjid forbear because the carrion lies under
> the shadow of the Ghor Kuttri? The matter began across
> the Border. It shall finish where God pleases. Here, in my
> country, or in Hell. All three are one.

$$(4\ 9-10)$$

Similarly in 'The Limitations of Pambe Serang' (1889) the
Malay serang who 'does not forget anything' hunts a Zanzibar
stoker half way across the world; he does not rest until his
victim is delivered into his hands.

Here it may not be out of place to mention that besides
India, the United States of America is also for Kipling a
symbol of anarchy and lawlessness. This picture of America
comes out very sharply in his record of his journey to the
States published in *From Sea to Sea*. In the boat a candid
American confesses:

> The more power you give the people, the more trouble
> they will give. With us our better classes are corrupt and
> our lower classes are *lawless*. There are millions of useful,
> law-abiding citizens, and they are very sick of this thing.
> We execute our justice in the streets. The law courts are no
> use.

$$(16\ 30.\ \text{Italics mine.})$$

In the Chinese quarter of San Francisco Kipling is himself
a witness to a murder committed in broad daylight. Democracy becomes a farce and another version of lawlessness.
Votes are bought and sold; tough gangs are used to influence
people in casting their votes. Likewise the public offices are
distributed according to political leanings, and thereby
officials become incapable of enforcing any regulations which
may be contrary to the interest of their voters:

> The Commissioner of Police has been helped to his post
> very largely by the influence of the boys [that is, gangs of
> hooligans] at such and such a saloon. He may be the
> guardian of city morals, but he is not going to allow his

subordinates to enforce early closing or abstention from gambling in that saloon.

(16 61)

In another section of his travel sketches, Kipling talks in memorable words about the disorder that is rampant in the States:

So long as they [that is, Americans in general] do not absolutely march into the District of Columbia, sit on the Washington statues, and invent a flag of their own, they can legislate, lynch, hunt negroes through swamps, divorce, railroad, and rampage as much as they choose. They do not need knowledge of their own military strength to back their genial *lawlessness*.

(16 191. Italics mine.)

Further on he comments that the Americans are 'Cock-sure . . . lawless and as casual as they are cocksure.'

Besides her adverse weather, death, decay, disease, darkness, ghosts, evil spirits and disorder, India makes one feel her hostility and malignancy in more subtle, psychologically crushing ways. One is the utter isolation to which India condemns her victims, especially the English. The loneliness of four young men in 'At the End of the Passage' is a good example:

They were lonely folk who understood the dread meaning of loneliness. They were all under thirty years of age, — which is too soon for any man to possess that knowledge.

(5 330)

In the story 'The Judgement of Dungara' (1888) there is another pertinent comment on the loneliness of Europeans:

There is only the isolation that weighs upon the waking eyelids and drives you perforce headlong into the labours of the day. There is no post, there is no one of your own colour to speak to, there are no roads: there is, indeed, food to keep you alive, but it is not pleasant to eat; and whatever of good and beauty and interest there is in your life, must come from yourself and the grace that may be planted in you.

(4 47)

Malignant India, moreover, makes it impossible for Anglo-Indians to establish human relationship with the natives. There is something in the very air in India, Kipling seems to suggest, that poisons all efforts at communication with Indians, and this evil influence is particularly seen in the tragic love affairs between Englishmen and Indian girls. Lispeth's affair with the young Englishman comes to nought, and with tears in her eyes she goes back to her own people. Perhaps, one might claim in this particular case, the young man did not love Lispeth. But in 'Beyond the Pale' (1888) we have a genuine love affair between Trejago, an Englishman, and Bisesa, a young Hindu widow whom he meets in a fairy-tale--like atmosphere. The relationship, when discovered, results in the cutting off of the girl's hands and the stabbing of Trejago.

This particular theme is treated with great sensitivity in 'Without Benefit of Clergy' (1890). The highly moving tragedy of Holden and Ameera is staged against the backdrop of India's silent malignant power that appears in the shape of cholera. The title refers, of course, to an illicit relation, but as Alan Sandison points out 'benefit of clergy' is also a technical phrase originally alluding to the exemption of ecclesiastics from secular jurisdiction.[17] It is thus clear that there is to be no exemption here — even for the lovers, for all the purity of their emotions. At the birth of their child Ameera rejoices that there is ' "a bond and a heel-rope between us now that nothing can break" ', but this bond snaps abruptly as Tota dies of 'the seasonal autumnal fever'. Later, cholera breaks out and snatches away even Ameera from Holden's arms.

Kipling's complex vision of India is perhaps most effectively suggested in a brief episode in 'At the End of the Passage'. When Hummil dies one can see that 'in the staring eyes was written terror beyond the expression of any pen'. Hummil has been 'seven fathom deep in hell' and has experienced horror of which there can be no account.

D KIPLING'S SOLUTION: EMPIRE BASED ON SERVICE AND SACRIFICE

India, an entity separate from Indians, is thus seen by Kipling as a monstrous being, restless and bewildering, an embodiment of Darkness, Chaos and Disorder which remains a constant challenge to the positive forces of Light, Order and Law. With his historical imagination Kipling seems to argue that the Aryans first conquered this land but they were subjugated by the Dark Forces; then came the Greeks, but even Alexander the Great failed to affix any pattern on India; the Muslims struggled with these negative forces for almost ten centuries without much success; and now it is the turn of the Anglo-Saxons to perform the God-given duty of making order prevail:

> We were dreamers, dreaming greatly, in the man-stifled
> town;
> We yearned beyond the sky-line where the strange roads
> go down.
> Came the Whisper, came the Vision, came the Power with
> the Need,
> Till the Soul that is not man's soul was lent us to lead.
> ('The Song of the Dead' (1893), *DE* 172)

As Dobrée points out, one must note that the Power was lent, not given, to the English to lead the world.[18] This is a very important observation, for Kipling was acutely conscious of a deeper purpose behind the Empire: he never failed to warn that the English would be deprived of this trust the moment they forgot that they were only agents in the hands of a higher power which was using them for the promulgation of the Law.

This view of Britain and her destiny under the Law was no mere theory to Kipling. The Empire was a practical living fact, and it contained within itself the germs of the true Imperial Idea. Nobody would suggest that the British Empire was based on altruistic ideals, yet the fact remains that the British did prove to be agents of progress in the world. Kipling saw that the British flag brought with it law, literacy, communications, medical facilities and useful arts. This is what he applauded, not the enlargement of frontiers. The true justification of the Empire was not a jingoistic national pride but 'a humble and a contrite heart':

Keep ye the Law — be swift in all obedience —
Clear the land of evil, drive the road and bridge the ford.
  Make ye sure to each his own
  That he reap where he hath sown;
By the peace among Our peoples let men know we serve
  the Lord!

('A Song of the English' (1893), *DE* 170)

The Law that the Empire-builder is commanded to keep is an equivalent of peace, order, justice and public works. In an early comment from New York in 'Across a Continent' (1892) Kipling says: 'In a heathen land the three things that are supposed to be pillars of moderately decent government are regard for human life, justice criminal and civil, as far as it lies in a man to do justice, and good roads.' (28 20) 'Judson and the Empire (1893) expresses scorn for the — unnamed — Portuguese Empire in East Africa:

> They had built no roads. Their towns were rotting under their hands; they had no trade worth the freight of a crazy steamer; and their sovereignty ran almost one musket-shot inland when things were peaceful.
>
> (3 530)

In India he saw that the British were driving the road and bridging the ford — something which was very dear to his heart:

> Year by year England sends out fresh drafts for the first fighting-line, which is officially called the Indian Civil Service. These die, or kill themselves by overwork, or are worried to death, or broken in health and hope in order that the land may be protected from death and sickness, famine and war, and may eventually become capable of standing alone. It will never stand alone, but the idea is a pretty one, and men are willing to die for it, and yearly the work of pushing and coaxing and scolding the country into good living goes forward.
>
> (4 305—6)

In *Egypt of the Magicians* (1913), he talks about his impressions of the British work in the Sudan:

The men who remember the old days of the Reconstruction — which deserves an epic of its own — say that there was nothing left to build on, not even wreckage. Knowledge, decency, kinship, property, title, sense of possession had all gone. The people were told they were to sit still and obey orders; and they stared and fumbled like dazed crowds after an explosion. . . . And little by little, as they realized that the new order was sure and that their ancient oppressors were quite dead, there returned not only cultivators, craftsmen, and artisans, but outlandish men of war, scarred with old wounds and the generous dimples that the Martini-Henry bullet used to deal — fighting men on the look-out for new employ.

(28 322)

In Canada this work of regeneration takes a different shape:

'Asphalt streets and concrete sidewalks came up a few years ago,' said our host as we trotted over miles of it. 'We found it the only way to fight the prairie mud. Look!' Where the daring road ended, there lay unsubdued, level with the pale asphalt, the tenacious prairie, over which civilisation fought her hub-deep way to the West. And with the asphalt and concrete they fight the prairie back every season.

(28 202–3)

The battle and building imagery of these passages is worth noting. Kipling speaks of the English Civil Servants in India — the upholders of the Imperial Idea — as the first fighting line against the Dark Forces which bring death, sickness, famine and war to humanity at large. Towards the end of the second passage above (4 305–6) the emphasis shifts from fighting to reconstruction of the country. In the passage about the Sudan (28 322) the same concern with heroic struggle against the negative forces and the rebuilding of order out of disorder is underlined by the words evoking battle and reconstruction: 'epic', 'explosion', 'outlandish men of war', 'scarred', 'old wounds' and 'bullet' conjure up the heroic fight against the forces of *nada* (Spanish for 'nothing'), while the process of reconstruction is suggested by 'build', 'the new order', 'cultivators, craftsmen, and artisans'. It is especially in the last quotation above (28 202—3) that the two-fold nature of the Imperial Idea, namely the battle against the negative forces and the establishment of a new order, is skilfully suggested through the imagery of battle and building. The tenacious, muddy prairie symbolises the Dark Powers. These Powers are opposed by the upholder of the Law that includes the Imperial Idea. The struggle is represented through the imagery of road-building with which the Empire-builder fights the prairie back.

The driving of the road and the bridging of the ford are such absorbing duties that one can hardly have any time to think about philosophical problems. Thus we are told in 'The Conversion of Aurelian McGoggin' (1887):

> Life, in India, is not long enough to waste in proving that there is no one in particular at the head of affairs. For this reason, the Deputy is above the Assistant, the Commissioner above the Deputy, the Lieutenant-Governor above the Commissioner, and the Viceroy above all four, under the orders of the Secretary of State who is responsible to the Empress. If the Empress be not responsible to her Maker — if there is no Maker for her to be responsible to — the entire system of Our administration must be wrong; which is manifestly impossible.
> (1 127—8)

These statements, along with Kipling's conviction of the British right to rule in India and elsewhere, prompt the question whether he asserted the superiority of the British race. The element of national pride is certainly very obvious in Kipling, but it is not blind nationalism and never degenerates to racism. Perhaps the question whether the Indians were unfit to rule themselves was irrelevant for Kipling: he would answer only by a statement — it was the mission of the British to rule and serve — a necessity imposed upon England by some organic determinism:

> *Fair is our lot — O goodly is our heritage!*
> *(Humble ye, my people, and be fearful in your mirth!)*
> *For the Lord our God Most High*
> *He hath made the deep as dry,*
> *He hath smote for us a pathway to the ends of all the Earth!*
> ('A Song of the English' (1893), *DE* 170)

And the satisfaction of fulfilling the Law is sufficient reward in itself. There is however a touch of complacency and arrogance in these lines — sins against which he is himself warning his people. The God Kipling is addressing is essentially a tribal deity who 'hath smote for us a pathway', yet this pride is tempered with the strong sense of duty, service and humility which comes out more sharply in the fourth stanza (quoted in Chapter 1, Section B). The pursuit of this duty often involves absolute self-sacrifice:

> We must feed our sea for a thousand years,
>   For that is our doom and pride,
> As it was when they sailed with the *Golden Hind,*
>   Or the wreck that struck last tide —
> Or the wreck that lies on the spouting reef
>   Where the ghastly blue-lights flare.
> If blood be the price of admiralty,
> If blood be the price of admiralty,
> If blood be the price of admiralty,
>   Lord God, we ha' bought it fair!
>   ('The Song of the Dead' (1893), *DE* 174)

The well-known poem 'The White Man's Burden' (1899) is worth close examination for the way in which it explicitly sets forth Kipling's views on the role of the Empire-builder in the world. The phrase 'White Man's Burden' has now become so hackneyed that it has lost its original meaning. In this connection it should be kept in mind that Kipling habitually wrote verses in contemporary colloquial language, and in the 1890s the phrase 'a white man', Carrington suggests, did not only mean a man with a white skin, it had a secondary symbolic meaning: 'a man with the moral standards of the civilized world'.[19] Thus in the oft-quoted ballad 'Gunga Din' (1890) Kipling gives a cockney soldier's comment on an Indian water-carrier, 'the finest man I knew':

> An' for all 'is dirty 'ide
> 'E was white, clear white, inside.
>   (*DE* 407)

Kipling firmly believed that it was the responsibility of the leading nations of the world to shape the destiny of 'fluttered folk and wild'. It was a burden involving sacrifice:

> Take up the White Man's burden —
>   Send forth the best ye breed —
> Go bind your sons to exile
>   To serve your captives' need.
>   (*DE* 323)

The task could only be performed by one who has the qualities of patience, humility and kindness:

> Take up the White Man's burden —
>   In patience to abide,
> To veil the threat of terror
>   And check the show of pride;
> By open speech and simple,
>   An hundred times made plain,
> To seek another's profit,
>   And work another's gain.
>   (*DE* 323)

Instead of bringing pomp and show Empire-building meant continuous hard work:

> Take up the White Man's burden —
>   No tawdry rule of kings,
> But toil of serf and sweeper —
>   The tale of common things.
>   (*DE* 324)

It was a duty to be done without the promise of material reward or even hope of success:

> Take up the White Man's burden —
>   And reap his old reward:
> The blame of those ye better,
>   The hate of those ye guard —
>
>   . . .
>
> And when your goal is nearest
>   The end for others sought,
> Watch Sloth and heathen Folly
>   Bring all your hope to nought.
>   (*DE* 324)

The only satisfaction that the Empire-builder could have was that perhaps the deed was worth doing for its own sake:

> Take up the White Man's burden —
> Have done with childish days —
> The lightly proffered laurel,
> The easy, ungrudged praise.
> Comes now, to search your manhood
> Through all the thankless years,
> Cold-edged with dear-bought wisdom.
> The judgment of your peers!
> (*DE* 324)

There are certain tones in this poem, as in 'The Song of the English', which suggests that Kipling was proud of the White Man's achievements, yet there would appear to be nothing wrong with having a sense of pride in something worthy and noble. The description of the natives — 'new-caught, sullen peoples,/Half devil and half child' — seems rather rash in its sweeping generalisation, but the poem is concerned with the definition of the task of the upholder of the Imperial Idea in areas where the people, not necessarily coloured, are under the sway of the Dark Powers.

'Recessional' (1897), published some eighteen months earlier than 'The White Man's Burden' though written at about the same time, shows similar features. The poem with its solemn movement and psalm echoes has a conscious humility and an unconscious arrogance. Kipling here addresses the 'Lord of our far-flung battle-line,' the adjective 'far-flung' implying the vastness of the British Empire, an impression strengthened by the sweeping 'dominion over palm and pine'. But the emphasis is on humility not pride:

> Far-called, our navies melt away;
> On dune and headland sinks the fire:
> Lo, all our pomp of yesterday
> Is one with Nineveh and Tyre!
> Judge of the Nations, spare us yet,
> Lest we forget — lest we forget!

> If, drunk with sight of power, we loose
> Wild tongues that have not Thee in awe,
> Such boastings as the Gentiles use,
> Or lesser breeds without the Law —
> Lord God of Hosts, be with us yet,
> Lest we forget — lest we forget!
>
> (*DE* 329)

The line 'Or lesser breeds without the Law' has been often used by Kipling's critics to prove that he was a narrow-minded imperialist, but there is no justification in supposing that 'lesser breeds' refers to subject native races or even coloured races: indeed the syntax of these lines proves that the lesser breeds are those nations who boast with 'wild tongues' having been 'drunk with sight of power'. Moreover, natives frequently command respect in his stories. Even though the European is often represented as a wise and benevolent leader of the world, there is rarely any suggestion of contempt for the native. The meaning of the first two words is completed by the last three: the breeds are 'lesser' because they are 'without the Law'. There is room for all within the Law, which sees no breed that has accepted it as greater or lesser than another. Those who hold the Law — that is, those who by disciplined effort are furthering the cause of civilization and are therefore trying to fulfil the world-purpose, are superior to those who are outside the Law. In other words the 'lesser breeds' are any races, irrespective of colour, caste or creed, who lack humility and an understanding of this discipline and purpose of life and who, in arrogance and vainglory, ignore the common good in the pursuit of selfish ends.

It must be kept in mind that 'Recessional' appeared in 1897 on the occasion of the second Jubilee. It was Britain's proudest moment in history and it is a tribute to Kipling that he could call on humility at this particular time. In *Something of Myself* Kipling says that the complacency and self-confidence shown by the English at the Diamond Jubilee disturbed him. He wrote 'Recessional' as a *nuzzur-wattu* (Panjabi for an 'averter of the Evil Eye'). (36 141)

Nothing is therefore farther from the truth than to accuse Kipling of fascism, racism or jingo imperialism. He was capable of recognising that the English were not without imperfections. In 'Tods' Amendment' (1887) Kipling candidly writes about the Indian Government's ignorance of the conditions of its subjects. The Legal Member would have passed a bill which would have adversely affected the local population had it not been for young Tods who had a perfect understanding of the natives' point of view. In 'The Masque of Plenty' (1888) Kipling bitterly criticizes the British Government for setting up committees to investigate Indian conditions. They are official and formal, interested only in speeding up the inquiry and then hurrying off to cool Simla:

> What is the state of the Nation? What is its occupation?
> Hi! Get along, get along, get along — lend us the
> information,
>
> (*DE* 35)

but the condition of the poor Indian farmer does not change a bit despite all these investigations:

> At his heart is his daughter's wedding,
> In his eye foreknowledge of debt.
> He eats and hath indigestion,
> He toils and may not stop;
> His life is a long-drawn question
> Between a crop and a crop.
>
> (*DE* 39)

Similarly Kipling's picture of the debauched social life of Anglo-Indians in Simla is certainly not complacent. His Anglo-Indian world is in many ways sordid and monotonous, a place where one can see little tin gods in their human frailty.

Kipling realised that the East had in some ways a better religion than the West: it was for this reason that he strongly opposed Christian missionary work in India. Kipling perhaps shared Mahbub Ali's attitude to religion when the horse-dealer says to Kim: ' "This matter of creeds is like horse-flesh. . . . Therefore I say in my heart the Faiths are like the horses. Each has merit in its own country." ' (*Kim* 19 234) *Kim* shows a great respect for the faith of the Lama, while in the same book Kipling speaks scornfully of the Protestant

parson, Bennett, who calls non-Christians 'heathen'. The con-
version of the pagan worshippers of Dungara comes to a
disastrous end in 'The Judgment of Dungara' (1888), where
the heroine is maltreated and lied to by the Chaplain of the
Kotgarh Mission and his wife, who seem to have no sympathy
or understanding. 'It takes a great deal of Christianity,'
Kipling comments sardonically, 'to wipe out uncivilised
Eastern instincts, such as falling in love at first sight.' (1 1)
The epigraph of this story shows Kipling's attitude to
Christianity in India:

> Look, you have cast out Love! What Gods are these
> 　　You bid me please?
> The Three in One, the One in Three? Not so!
> 　　To my own Gods I go.
> It may be they shall give me greater ease
> Than your cold Christ and tangled Trinities.
>
> 　　　　　　　　　　　　　(*The Convert*, 1 1)

Kipling was also capable of recognising the worth of the
natives and at times he frankly admits their superiority over
the English. Gunga Din is a better man than the average
Tommy; and the Sudanese Fuzzy Wuzzy are worthy of admiration as excellent fighters. In 'The Ballad of East and
West' (1899) Kipling sings of the nobility and heroism of
Kamal, a fierce Pathan freebooter, who becomes a blood
brother of the Colonel's son:

> They have looked each other between the eyes, and
> 　　there they found no fault.
> They have taken the Oath of the Brother-in-Blood on
> 　　leavened bread and salt:
> They have taken the Oath of the Brother-in-Blood on
> 　　fire and fresh-cut sod,
> On the hilt and the haft of the Khyber knife, and the
> 　　Wondrous Names of God.
>
> 　　　　　　　　　　　　　(*DE* 237)

And Kipling goes on to comment that there is no difference
between two strong men when they meet face to face:

Oh, East is East, and West is West, and never the
  twain shall meet,
Till Earth and Sky stand presently at God's great
  Judgement Seat;
But there is neither East nor West, Border, nor Breed,
  nor Birth,
When two strong men stand face to face, though they
  come from the ends of the earth!
                                                    (*DE* 238)

Sir Purun Dass, K.C.I.E., the Prime Minister of a native state who appears in the story 'The Miracle of Purun Bhagat' (1894), is represented as being a discreet, firm and tactful administrator. Similarly Mr Grish Chunder De is quite successful in his own district of Bengal. These examples disprove the argument that Kipling condemns all Indian natives as unfit to rule.

Kipling was indeed a severe critic of the British Government. And yet his case for the presence of the British regime in India and elsewhere was that, with all its imperfections, it was the best system the undeveloped countries had or were likely to have. As suggested earlier this conviction was based on the reconstruction done by the English in the colonies.

Kipling was conscious of the fact that the Empire was not eternal and that, as we have said, the English would lose it the moment they neglected their moral duty. 'The Man who would be King' (1888) illustrates the point amply. Daniel Dravot dreams of an empire, founds one in Kafiristan, a remote area on the North West frontier, and proves to be a beneficent ruler for a while. However the conception of the empire gets too big for him and he 'cracks'. His demands for a wife result in the destruction of Dravot's superhuman image, and he loses both his head and the kingdom. The moral of the story is that what can happen in Kafiristan may happen to *pax Britannica*. The duty assigned to the Empire-builder may be beyond human powers; yet the Empire-builder must try to fulfil this divine mission to the best of his ability: otherwise he will meet Dravot's fate.

Kipling envisaged something similar to the Commonwealth as the future shape of the Empire: a number of independent nations bound together by a community of purpose and ad-

vanced means of communication.[20] Speaking to the Canadian
Club at Toronto in 1907 he explained:

> I have, I confess it now, done my best for about twenty
> years to make all men of the sister nations within the
> Empire interested in each other. Because I know that at
> heart all our men are pretty much alike, in that they have
> the same aspirations, and the same loves, and the same
> hates; and when all is said and done we have only each
> other to depend upon.
>
> (32 37—8)

In 1925 he announced at a Chamber of Shipping dinner:

> Everywhere time and space are coming to heel round us to
> fetch and carry for our behoof, in the wilderness or the
> market. And that means that it will be possible for us now,
> as never before to fuse our Empire together in thought and
> understanding as closely as in the interchange of men and
> things.
>
> (32 288)

In two stories written in his middle period, 'With the Night
Mail' (1910) and 'As Easy as A.B.C' (1912), the organisation
of transport and traffic on which all other activities depend is
the only defined function of an effective government. The
stories picture the world under the ultimate control of an
international body, the Aerial Board of Control. In the light-
hearted 'With the Night Mail', set in A.D. 2000, Kipling explains that the A.B.C. is:

> . . . that semi-elected, semi-nominated body of a few score
> persons of both sexes, that controls this planet. 'Transpor-
> tation is Civilisation', our motto runs. Theoretically we do
> what we please so long as we do not interfere with the
> traffic *and all it implies.* Practically, the A. B. C. confirms
> or annuls all international arrangements and, to judge from
> its last report, finds our tolerant, humourous, lazy little
> planet only too ready to shift the whole burden of public
> administration on its shoulders.
>
> (26 3)

The world pictured in these stories is not altogether attractive, but Kipling seems to present the A.B.C. as a reasonable solution to the world's complex problems. This international body is in a way an objectification of the idea of Empire for it brings the entire globe into discipline and order under a universal law.

Thus we see that Kipling's concept of Empire is a much deeper concept than is generally recognised. Essentially Empire stands for the forces of law, order and discipline which are engaged in a constant struggle against the negative forces of chaos, confusion and disorder. So Kipling's imperial drama assumes the proportions of a morality play in a non-theological sense. This pattern is well illustrated by 'The Bridge-Builders' (1893). The dusky goddess India, as suggested in Section C above, symbolises the Dark Powers. Empire stands for the Forces of Light. The struggle is for the possession of Indians who represent humanity at large.

The struggle between the Good and Evil Forces in 'The Bridge-Builders' is symbolised by the bridge-building over the Ganges that has been going on for three years in spite of every conceivable obstruction. Incessant toil at last makes the black frame of the Kashi Bridge rise plate by plate, girder by girder, span by span. Old Peroo knows that Mother Gunga cannot take this bridling any more, and sure enough Gunga wakes up in all her fury. The great flood comes, and Findlayson and Peroo drift to a little island where they rest near a Hindu shrine. Both men are drugged, and at this stage the tale passes into their trance. They witness a *punchayet* (meeting) of the Indian gods.

Mother Gunga starts speaking with the complaint: ' "They have chained my flood, and my river is not free any more. . . .Deal me the justice of the Gods!" ' Indra does not like the impatience of Gunga: ' "The deep sea was where she runs but yesterday, and tomorrow the sea shall cover her again as the Gods count that which men call time. Can any one say that their bridge endures till tomorrow?" ' Gunga repeats: ' "They have changed the face of the land — which is my land. They have killed and made new towns on my banks." ' Ganesha tries to calm her down by arguing: ' "It is but the shifting of a little dirt. Let the dirt dig in the dirt if it pleases the dirt." ' Hanuman adds: ' "Ho! Ho! I am the

builder of bridges indeed — bridges between this and that,
and each bridge leads surely to Us in the end. Be content,
Gunga. Neither these men nor those that follow them mock
thee at all." ' Once again Indra sums up the case: ' "Ye know
the Riddle of the Gods. When Brahm ceases to dream the
Heavens and the Hells and the Earth disappear. Be content.
Brahm dreams still. The dreams come and go, and the nature
of the dreams changes, but Brahm still dreams. . . . The Gods
change, beloved — all save One." '

This is the riddle. All is *maya* (illusion) — nothing remains.
The toil and trouble of the men working for sweetness and
light come to nought in the ultimate analysis. The Kashi
Bridge may be spared by the gods today, but tomorrow it
will be washed away by angry Gunga:

> Cities and Thrones and Powers
>   Stand in Time's eye,
> Almost as long as flowers,
>   Which daily die:
> But, as new buds put forth
>   To glad new men,
> Out of the spent and unconsidered Earth
>   The Cities rise again.
>
> This season's Daffodil,
>   She never hears
> What change, what chance, what chill
>   Cut down last year's;
> But with bold countenance,
>   And knowledge small,
> Esteems her seven days' continuance
>   To be perpetual.
>
> So Time that is o'er-kind
>   To all that be,
> Ordains us e'en as blind,
>   As bold as she:
> That in our very death,
>   And burial sure,
> Shadow to shadow, well persuaded, saith,
>   'See how our works endure!'
>   (' "Cities and Thrones and Powers" ', *DE* 487)

Such is the mystery of this world. Yet in spite of an awareness of final defeat Kipling exhorts men to accept the challenge and put up a heroic fight against the forces of *nada* (nothing). The odds may be against him but the final result does not matter. Man's victory lies in the struggle which he puts up against darkness, chaos and disorder. In the ultimate analysis Kipling's is a very positive message.

5 The Doctrine of Action

First a man must suffer, then he must learn his work, and the self-respect that that knowledge brings.

'The Strange Ride of Morrowbie Jukes', 5 214

A SUFFERING AND ACTION

In his address to the students of McGill University delivered on 23 October 1907 Kipling warned:

> There is a certain darkness into which the soul of the young man sometimes descends – a horror of desolation, abandonment, and realised worthlessness, which is one of the most real of the hells in which we are compelled to walk.
> I know of what I speak. . . . But I can tell you for your comfort that the best cure for it is to interest yourself, to lose yourself, in some issue not personal to yourself – in another man's trouble, or, preferably, another man's joy. . . . In other words, take anything and everything seriously except yourselves.
>
> (32 24–5)

Almost the whole of Kipling's philosophy can be discussed from this text: realisation of the meaninglessness of life, disinterested suffering and the need for positive action form the crux of Kipling's thought. As shown in the previous chapter Kipling's imperial drama revolves around this very doctrine of suffering and action, so that his imperialistic theme takes on a secondary importance only.

Kipling's universe, as indicated by his vision of India, is essentially indifferent or hostile towards man. There is a deity, Kipling seems to suggest, hidden somewhere in the clouds so we cannot see it, which is perhaps good for man:

> A veil 'twixt us and Thee, Good Lord,
>   A veil 'twixt us and Thee:
> Lest we should hear too clear, too clear,
>   And unto madness see!
> > ('The Prayer of Miriam Cohen', *DE* 614)

But fact remains that the Dark Powers reign supreme in this world; they frustrate man's every effort at putting an order and a pattern upon the existing chaos. At every turn Kipling encounters these dark, nameless and shapeless powers, which throw him deep down into the abyss of nothingness:

> A stone's throw out on either hand
> From that well-ordered road we tread,
> And all the world is wild and strange: . . .
> Wherein the Powers of Darkness range.
>   of Darkness range.
> > (1 159)

At the age of twenty Kipling had, in what he describes as a 'pivot' experience, the first serious encounter with the Powers of Darkness:

> It happened one hot-weather evening, in '86 or there-abouts, when I felt that I had come to the edge of all endurance. As I entered my empty house in the dusk there was no more in me except the horror of a great darkness, that I must have been fighting for some days. I came through that darkness alive, but how I do not know.
> > (36 63–4)

Years later Kipling was seized with the same horror of darkness as he entered the house in Torquay on his return from the United States:

> The other revelation came in the shape of a growing depression which enveloped us both — a gathering blackness of mind and sorrow of the heart . . . It was Feng-shui — the Spirit of the house itself — that darkened the sunshine and fell upon us every time we entered, checking the very words on our lips.
> > (36 129)

It was here that Kipling felt a 'brooding Spirit of deep, deep Despondency'. (36 130)

This mood of deep despondency is strongly reflected in Kipling's writings; the note of despair becomes even more poignant in his later career. Through the narrator of 'The House Surgeon' (1909), the last tale in *Actions and Reactions,* Kipling speaks of how 'my amazed and angry soul dropped gulf by gulf into that horror of great darkness which is spoken of in the Bible . . . despair upon despair, misery upon misery, fear after fear. . . .' (24 288) This mood of black despair often appears in Kipling's writings in the form of war neurosis and breaking strain, which remain his preoccupations till the very end of his career.[1]

Marden and Martin Ballart, who appear in two tales of his last volume *Limits and Renewals* (1932), are examples of those men 'whom the War had immobilised from the soul outwards'. (33 351) In 'The Miracle of Saint Jubanus' (1930) the narrator makes a succinct comment on the psychological effect of the War:

> I saw them, after the War, split open! Some entered hells of whose existence they had not dreamed — of whose terrors they lacked words to tell.
>
> (33 350—1)

Too much strain and pressure produce the same state of mind. In a very late poem, 'Hymn of Breaking Strain' (1935), Kipling's heart goes out to the afflicted man whom the gods kill for their sport:

> The careful text-books measure
> (Let all who build beware!)
> The load, the shock, the pressure
> Material can bear.
> So, when the buckled girder
> Lets down the grinding span,
> The blame of loss, or murder,
> Is laid upon the man.
> *Not on the Stuff — the Man!*

> But, in our daily dealing
>   With stone and steel, we find
> The Gods have no such feeling
>   Of justice toward mankind.
> To no set gauge they make us, —
>   For no laid course prepare —
> And presently o'ertake us
>   With loads we cannot bear:
>   *Too merciless to bear.*
>   (*DE* 384)

In Kipling's world, generally speaking, man and his works remain bits of dirt, shiftings of dirt which are blown down the *khud* (hillside) in no time. This is what Ganesh says in *The Bridge-Builders* (1893) — all is *maya* — we exist in the dream of Brahma only. This amounts to philosophic nihilism on Kipling's part. Rider Haggard records that once when he was talking with Kipling 'I happened to remark that I thought this was one of the hells. He replied that he did not *think,* he was *certain* of it.'[2]

Nevertheless these nihilistic tendencies do not lead Kipling to escapism, which is precisely what makes his thought so complex. Despite his acute awareness of the fact that the Forces of Darkness remain undefeated, Kipling believes in the existence of a greater Power — 'the veiled and secret Power' — that can provide an anodyne for the dark hours. Towards the end of the poem 'Hymn of Breaking Strain' Kipling turns to this 'veiled and secret Power' for succour against the gods who 'o'ertake us/With loads we cannot bear':

> Oh, veiled and secret Power
>   Whose paths we seek in vain,
> Be with us in our hour
>   Of overthrow and pain;
> That we — by which sure token
>   We know Thy ways are true —
> In spite of being broken,
>   *Because of being broken,*
>   *May rise and build anew.*
>   *Stand up and build anew!*
>   (*DE* 385)

Suffering, defeat and pain can make one who knows the ways of this Power take up the challenge and fight against the lesser gods with renewed energy. Thus man may rise and build anew. The emphasis, it may be noted, is on building, reconstruction and ceaseless work which may bring a sense of self-fulfilment to the already vanquished man.

The universe may be malignant and hostile yet Kipling believes that man, and man alone, is responsible for his own destiny, and that he can make his own hell or heaven on this earth. That statement may sound self-contradictory but it is precisely, as Professor Dobrée remarks, on such seemingly incompatible foundations that Kipling builds his philosophy of life.[3] Kipling seems to suggest that although man is ultimately destined to be defeated by the Dark Powers, he has two choices: either to let himself be devoured by the Dark Powers, or through suffering and action to bring himself out of the limbo of nothingness and thereby preserve his individuality. Man, according to Kipling, has no reality beyond his own actions: man *is* what he *does;* there is no ideal or essence in man which exists independently of action, and work is not only a means of ameliorating man's existence in a hostile universe but the very existence itself.

Perhaps the most complete statement of this philosophy is contained in 'The Children of the Zodiac' (1891), the first of Kipling's multi-layered fables, and so a detailed analysis of the story is imperative for our purposes.

'The Children of the Zodiac', which has echoes of Milton's *Paradise Lost* and Keats's *The Fall of Hyperion,* is a myth of self-knowledge which goes through negative capability, disinterested suffering and positive action. Kipling, it may be noted, was a great admirer of both Milton and Keats: M'Turk vouches for his interest in the two poets while he was at school.[4]

The story introduces us to the god-like symbols of the Powers of Light, the Children of the Zodiac — Leo, the Girl (Virgo), the Ram, the Bull and the Twins — who at the beginning of the tale, and by implication at the beginning of the world, are incapable of understanding human emotions though they are worshipped by humanity at large.

Opposed to these Powers of Light are the remaining signs

of the Zodiac, namely the Archer, the Scorpion, the Crab, the Scales, the Waterman and the Fishes, who symbolise the Dark Powers and who are interested only 'in killing man'. This dualism in the universe, an idea which is recurrent in Kipling's writings, indicates Zoroastrian influence on Kipling.[5]

The Children of the Zodiac who represent Good remain indifferent to the human plight for 'thousands of years by human reckoning', until on a particular day a change takes place: Leo meets the Girl walking across a hill and they both recognise that they have undergone 'startling changes'. Then 'Leo kissed the Girl, and all Earth felt that kiss' — recalling Milton's 'Earth felt the wound, and Nature from her Seat/ Sighing through all her works gave signs of woe/That all was lost'. (*Paradise Lost*, 9 782—4)[6]

Leo and the Girl lose their god-like status as well as the state of blissful ignorance, but at this terrible cost they do gain knowledge. (The parallel to the Fall of Adam and Eve is quite obvious here.) Besides knowledge the fall opens the door to human love — something which Leo and the Girl have never before experienced. Now they move to the next stage of their development — disinterested suffering — as they decide to taste death for the sake of humanity at large. The Children of the Zodiac, divested of the last vestiges of divinity, are now completely identified with mankind.

Along with knowledge and understanding the change in their status brings fear to the Children of the Zodiac. They feel that their lives are empty of meaning. Therefore, like men, all the Children of the Zodiac turn to work as the only way of controlling this fear and of giving their lives any meaning whatever. Leo and the Girl wander through the country and see the Bull plowing a straight furrow, doing the best work of which he is capable before his death. The Ram permits himself to be exhibited to villagers who had never seen a perfect ram, and the Twins pose as foundling babies, amusing a woman who likes them. Leo and Virgo become singers, entertaining people and helping them to forget their fear. The main theme of Leo's songs is the glorification of work and courage in the face of heavy odds — this is the role of the artist as Kipling conceives it.

Another story, 'Cold Iron' (1909) included in *Rewards and Fairies* (1910), bears close resemblance to 'The Children of the Zodiac'. It tells of a boy who is carried by Puck to fairyland where he is brought up by Sir Huon and Lady Esclairmonde. The boy's foster parents do not like his continued concern for the people of the mortal world; they make him promise that he will never go near men. But one day, required to find his own fortune on Puck's Hill, the boy finds the Cold Iron in the form of a slave ring, not, as his foster parents had hoped, in the shape of a king's sceptre or a knight's sword. And Puck explains what the fortune means for the boy:

> 'The virtue of the Ring is only that he must go among folk in housen henceforward, doing what they want done, or what he knows they need, all Old England over. Never will he be his own master, not yet ever any man's. He will get half he gives, and give twice what he gets, till his life's last breath; and if he lays aside his load before he draws that last breath, all his work will go for naught.'

(25 31)

The Cold Iron is thus a symbol of a life of toil and trouble that is lived for the sake of others without expectation of reward. A total indentification with the humble 'folk in housen', disinterested suffering and selfless work till the moment of death are the destiny of man under the Cold Iron. The Zodiac, which governs all the houses, good or evil, decrees the course of action that Leo and the Girl must follow in order to bring amelioration to humanity at large. This decreed path involves complete identification with suffering humanity, love and fearless action. The Cold Iron and the Zodiac symbolise stern necessity, another instrument of the Law. This ordained course of action is the only available means by which man may oppose the Dark Forces, and whereby he may attain a sense of self-fulfilment in a hostile universe.

This Law, as the very words 'the Cold Iron' suggest, is perhaps impersonal, stern and cruel. However one is free to follow or not to follow the Law. Leo and the Girl come down to the mortal world of their own free will. Similarly the boy, though he has found the Cold Iron, is free to throw it away and return to fairyland. But the boy has realized the meaninglessness of life in fairyland and like Leo he decides to choose the Cold Iron, though he knows very well the implications of such a decision. It is therefore clear from these two stories that three of the things that the Law requires for a meaningful existence in this indifferent universe are negative capability, suffering and action.

B MEN OF ACTION

Kipling was one of the first modern artists to write the epic of 'Tools and Man'. His world is chiefly composed of administrators, engineers, doctors, soldiers, railwaymen and peasants busy at their jobs. His writings are punctuated by the constant rhythms of everyday work. This is something which had been neglected by the literature of the past two centuries as an unworthy subject for art. And it was Kipling, as C. S. Lewis points out, who first reclaimed for literature this vast area of human activity.[7] It is therefore not surprising to learn that 'the most popular modern British poet in Moscow is Kipling'.[8]

' "I like men who do things," ' declares William the Conqueror, one of Kipling's heroines, to a man in the Education Department who was teaching the beauties of Wordsworth's 'Excursion' to Indian students. Comparable with this is Kipling's acknowledgement of 'the gulf that separates even the least of those who do things worthy to be written about from even the best of those who have written things worthy of being talked about'. (32 3) He recognizes the importance of the craft and magic of words, but the duty of 'the man with the Words' is to 'wait upon the man of achievement, and step by step with him try to tell the story of the Tribe' (32 7) — a pronouncement which throws a good deal of light on his own artistic intentions.

I will now consider in some detail the types of men of action whose 'story' is recorded by Kipling, 'the man with the Words'.

1 The Civil Servant

Kipling has been accused of a juvenile glorification of the English civil servant in India.[9] However Kipling's attitude to the civil servant is not as uniformly approving as one is led to believe by his critics, as we saw in references to 'The Masque of Plenty' and 'Tods' Amendment in the foregoing chapter. 'Pig' (1887) is another interesting example of Kipling's criticism of the impersonality, red tape and ignorance of the real problems on the part of the Anglo-Indian administration. The framework of 'Pig' is a revenge story, but it includes satire on the administrative conditions which alone make such a revenge possible. The story tells of an 'earnest' civil servant named Nafferton who informs the Indian Government that he has devised a scheme whereby a very large percentage of the British Army in India can be fed, at a very large saving, on pig. And therefore he requests the Government for 'varied information necessary to the proper inception of the scheme'. (1 240) The Indian Government instructs another 'earnest' civil servant named Pinecoffin to furnish the required information to Nafferton. Pinecoffin prepares a scholarly essay running into twenty-seven foolscap sheets on the ' "Primitive Pig, the Mythology of the Pig, and the Dravidian Pig" ', which he sends to Nafferton. Nafferton now wants to know the distribution of the pig in the Panjab, and how it stands the plains in the hot weather. Pinecoffin makes further laborious enquiries but before he can finish he is transferred on special duty to Kohat.

On his return from Kohat Pinecoffin, who has now developed a pig theory of his own, sends a report of thirty-three folio pages on the pig to Nafferton. However the process has taken about ten months, and at this stage Pinecoffin's interest in the 'potential Piggery' dies down. Nafferton, nevertheless, is quite serious about his pig theory; he now bombards Pinecoffin with letters on 'the Imperial aspect of the scheme, as tending to officialise the sale of pork, and thereby calculated to give offence to the Mohammedan population of Upper India'. (1 243) Pinecoffin replies that there is no such danger, in his opinion at least. Nafferton now gets interested in 'the possible profits to accrue to the Government from the sale of hog-bristles' (1 243), and he asks Pinecoffin to explore this possibility. Poor Pinecoffin visits Cawnpore factories and tanneries, and sends back a monograph of fifty-one pages on the ' "Products of the Pig" '. Nafferton now goes back to the second section of his fifth question: ' "How can the exotic pig be brought to give as much pork as it does in the West?" ' Pinecoffin replies: ' "Consult my first letter." ' This enrages Nafferton so much that he complains formally to the Government that he is not being given the required information. And the Government writes a stern letter to Pinecoffin telling him that 'the Service was made for the country, and not the country for the Service, and that he had better begin to supply information about Pigs'. (1 245)

The story is an obvious satire on the lack of constructiveness, impracticality and misapplication of energy and resources on the part of the administration. Kipling comments rather sardonically on these seemingly 'earnest' Anglo-Indian civil servants:

> I am not sure what real 'earnestness' is. A very fair imitation can be manufactured by neglecting to dress decently, by mooning about in a dreamy, misty sort of way, by taking office-work home after staying in the office till seven, and by receiving crowds of native gentlemen on Sundays. That is one sort of 'earnestness'.
>
> (1 240)

Similarly in 'The Bridge-Builders' (1893) Kipling attacks the civil service for red tape and impracticality. The Kashi Bridge is near completion when the Government of India adds two feet to its width, under the impression that bridges are cut out of paper, and so brings to ruin at least half an acre of calculations.

Another hint at governmental inefficiency and bureaucracy may be witnessed in 'William the Conqueror' (1895). Scott, who is in charge of relief work in a certain section of famine-stricken South India, pays the labourers from his own pocket trusting that he will be reimbursed later by the Government, for he knows that if he waits until the money comes from the state coffers the work will suffer:

Theoretically, the Government should have paid for every shoe and linchpin, for every hand employed in the loading; but Government vouchers cash themselves slowly, and intelligent and efficient clerks write at great length, contesting unauthorised expenditures of eight annas. The man who wishes to make his work a success must draw on his own bank-account of money or other things as he goes.

(13 259)

Kipling is also aware of the fact that positions in the civil service are often secured through influence, not merit. Mrs Hauksbee, the socialite of Simla, tells Otis Yeere:

'Look! There is young Hexarly with six years' service and half your talents. He asked for what he wanted, and he got it. See, down by the Convent! There's McArthurson, who has come to his present position by asking — sheer, downright asking — after he had pushed himself out of the rank and file. . . . Do you suppose men are chosen for appointments because of their special fitness *beforehand*?'

('The Education of Otis Yeere' (1888), 6 28)

And then there is the case of Tarrion who gets a position in the civil service because of the maneuvers of Mrs Hauksbee herself.

In the background of the Government lies the sordid Simla society with its social jealousies, midnight revelries and illicit affairs. The bureaucrats at Simla are inefficient: they are concerned only with preparing reports and setting up committees with no knowledge of what is going on in India.

In an uncollected poem 'Parturiunt Montes', which appeared in the *Civil and Military Gazette* on 26 April 1886 and in the *Pioneer* on 29 April 1886, Kipling draws a vivid picture of these good-for-nothing bureaucrats of Simla. The scene is laid in the Simla Offices where the chorus of members with their shirt-sleeves rolled up declares:

We are going to retrench! Yes! we're going to retrench.
   In a rigid revolutionary style;
From the Judge upon his Bench, on his costly-cushioned
   Bench

To the Babu and the Commissariat *Byle*!
. . . Let the fat Departments blench,
    We are yearning to retrench
In a clip and cut and skin-removing style! (Uncollected)[10]

Then the President steps in and says:

And I shall evolve a Report
    Shall write you a splendid Report;
And 'neath my direction each para and section
    Shall sparkle with jewels of thought!
Ye Gods! it must be a Report
    To set all the others at naught:
An elephant-folio, phototype-oleo;
    Guttenberg-Caxton Report![11]

A motion of moving 'in sign of unanimity' is carried, and *'the Hon'be W. W. — intones fortissimo through a paper trumpet'*:

Bring pens in sheaves and writing blocks in bales?
Pour out the ink-kegs into stable-pails!
Let blotting pads in bushels strew the floor!
Produce your office-boxes by the score!
Pile on statistics till the tables creak,
[E — t and I can sift 'em in a week]
Each to his place! Draw out your cleanest pen
Flourish it once, and — put it back again!
Drop down exhausted! Let the Public see
You're worth your salt! Now, taking time from me,
Wipe with one trembling hand a toil-worn brow —
Then, all together, *make an awful row!*
Turn to the Plains! What ho there! Pipes and tabors!
Tell them about our Herculean labours.[12]

Then the full chorus sings in harmony:

We're a wonderful Committee; we deserve your praise and
    pity,
Ke—ind Christian fellow-citizens we hope you'll take the
    hint.
We are dying of exertion and the lack of all diversion;
And should value the insertion of these sentiments in
    print.[13]

Kipling does not even spare the Viceroy, as we see in 'The Bridge-Builders':

> 'Ho! Ho! He is like the Burra Malum. He sleeps below while the work is being done. Then he comes upon the quarter-deck and touches with his finger, and says, "This is not clean!"'

(13 13)

These examples prove that Kipling is not guilty of unreserved adulation of the Anglo-Indian civil servant and that he does not make all of them heroes. The type of civil servant that Kipling admires is a man of strong character and honour who performs his responsibilities to the best of his ability under the most trying circumstances — a man for whom work assumes proportions larger than anything else and who consequently does his job with complete devotion.

In the tale 'At the End of the Passage' (1890) we meet four civil servants — Mottram, Lowndes, Spurstow and Hummil — who are scornful and sarcastic about everything in heaven and earth; but each in his own way in remote regions of the Empire is doing an arduous duty concerning the health and welfare of thousands, and despite the maddening heat, loneliness and fear, none of them will leave his post.

Orde is another example of Kipling's admired type of civil servant. He appears in 'The Enlightenments of Pagett, M.P.' (1890) as the Deputy-Commissioner of a North West Province which he administers with great sympathy and understanding. He can be approached by the humblest villager of his region without any difficulty. He is familiar with the real problems that are faced by the people; therefore he can afford to sneer at Pagett. Reappearing in 'The Head of the District' (1890) Orde, as he is dying, gives directions to relieve the poor villagers and to accelerate the work which will make the place more prosperous:

> 'It isn't that I mind dying,' he said. 'It's leaving Polly and the district. . . . That reminds me, Dick; the four Khusru Kheyl villages in our border want a one-third remittance this spring. That's fair; their crops are bad. See that they get it, and speak to Ferris about the canal. I should like to

have lived till that was finished; it means so much for the North-Indus villagers — but Ferris is an idle beggar — wake him up. . . . Call the Khusru Kheyl men up; I'll hold my last public audience. Khoda Dad Khan!'

(4 171–2)

The dying Deputy-Commissioner goes on to deliver his sermon to the villagers:

'. . . But you must be good men when I am not here. Such of you as live in our borders must pay your taxes quietly as before. I have spoken of the villages to be gently treated this year. Such of you as live in the hills must refrain from cattle-lifting, and burn no more thatch, and turn a deaf ear to the voice of the priests, who, not knowing the strength of the Government, would lead you into foolish wars, wherein you will surely die and your crops be eaten by strangers. And you must not sack any caravans, and must leave your arms at the police-post when you come in; as has been your custom, and my order. . . . I speak now true talk, for I am as it were already dead, my children, — for though ye be strong men, ye are children.'   *203714*

(4 172–3)

Tallantire, Orde's assistant, follows in his footsteps. After Orde's death the district is plunged into chaos as a result of Grish Chunder De's appointment. Tallantire however is able to restore law and order in the turbulent district of Kot-Kumharsen because of his understanding of the regional problems and the personal interest with which he carries out his duties.

Another of Kipling's civil servants, performing his duties silently in a remote corner of the Empire, is Gisborne of the Forest Department, the warden of the great *rukh* (jungle) which he loves as well as his forest rangers:

. . . the forests took him back again, and he was content to serve them, to deepen and widen his fire-lines, to watch the green mist of his new plantation against the old foliage, to dredge out the choked stream, and to follow and strengthen the last struggle of the forest where it broke down and died among the long pig-grass. . . . His bungalow,

a thatched white-walled cottage of two rooms, was set at
one end of the great *rukh* and overlooking it . . . the *rukh*
swept up to his door, curled over in a thicket of bamboo,
and he rode from his verandah into its heart without the
need of any carriage-drive.

(7 300—1)

When a ranger dies Gisborne pays his widow from his own
pocket 'a sum that the Government of India would never
have sanctioned for her man's death'. (7 303) On another
occasion a forest-guard is killed by a man-eating tiger and
Gisborne, guided by Mowgli, goes alone to shoot it, for he
feels responsible for the safety of the people in the *rukh*.

Kipling's admiration for a job done well without any expectation of reward comes out sharply in his comments on
the Forest Officers stationed in isolated corners of the
Empire:

Of the wheels of public service that turn under the Indian
Government, there is none more important than the
Department of Woods and Forests. . . . Its servants wrestle
with wandering sand-torrents and shifting dunes: wattling
them at the sides, damming them in front, and pegging them
down atop with coarse grass and spindling pine after the
rules of Nancy. . . . In th plains the chief part of their duty
is to see that the belt fire-lines in the forest reserves are kept
clean, so that when drought comes and the cattle starve, they
may throw the reserve open to the villager's herds and allow
the man himself to gather sticks. They poll and lop for the
stacked railway-fuel along the lines that burn no coal; they
calculate the profit of their plantations to five points of
decimals; they are the doctors and midwives of the hugh teak
forests of Upper Burma, the rubber of the Eastern Jungles,
and the gall-nuts of the South; and they are always hampered
by lack of funds.

(7 299)

In 'The Tomb of his Ancestors' (1897) we are introduced to the Chinn family which has produced capable
civil and military officers for the province of Bombay. John
Chinn the First goes into the country of the wild Bhils, lives

with them, protects them from leopards and tigers and wins their confidence. 'It was slow, unseen work, of the sort that is being done all over India today,' Kipling comments, supplying the key to the type of administrator that he admired. John Chinn dies serving the Bhils but the people do not forget him: they worship him as a local god. Years later John Chinn the Younger, who is an officer in the Bhil Regiment, has to use his ancestral image in order to persuade the Bhils to get themselves inoculated against smallpox.

Bakri Scott of the Punjab Civil Service lives up to the traditions of Kipling's ideal civil servant when he is placed at the disposal of the Madras Government for famine duty. Scott performs his task with such dedication and heroism that his boss expresses his impressions of Scott's achievements in these words:

> 'Look at this, Lizzie, for one week's work! Forty miles in two days with twelve carts; two days' halt building a famine-shed for young Rogers (Rogers ought to have built it himself, the idiot!). Then forty miles back again, loading six carts on the way, and distributing all Sunday. Then in the evening he pitches in a twenty-page demi-official to me, saying that the people where he is might be "advantageously employed on relief-work", and suggesting that he put 'em to work on some broken-down old reservoir he's discovered, so as to have a good water-supply when the Rains come.'

(13 259–60)

Similarly Kipling's ideal police officer is Strickland, who is completely dedicated to his job and who knows 'as much about the natives as the natives themselves'. He can pass for a Hindu or a Muslim, he explores the native riff-raff, he is initiated into the *Sat Bhai* at Allahabad, he knows the 'Lizzard Song' of the Sanyasis and 'the *Halli-Hukk* dance' of the mystics and he masters the thieves' patter of the *changars* (men of low caste). Often he takes leave for what he calls *shikar* (hunting), puts on the disguise that appeals to him at that time, steps down into the bazaar and is swallowed in the brown crowd. Strickland seems to be modelled after the *kotwal* (chief police officer) of the *Arabian Nights,* in which

the *kotwal* and Caliph Harun-al-Rashid often roam around
the streets of Baghdad in disguise to acquaint themselves with
the real condition of the people.

Perhaps Kipling's view of an ideal civil servant is best
summed up in the following passage (already quoted in Chapter 4 Section D):

> Year by year England sends out fresh drafts for the first
> fighting-line, which is officially called the Indian Civil Ser-
> vice. These die, or kill themselves by overwork, or are
> worried to death, or broken in health and hope in order
> that the land may be protected from death and sickness,
> famine and war, and may eventually become capable of
> standing alone.
>
> (4 305—6)

2 The Soldier

Kipling's admiration for the soldier has led to the charge that
he loved brutality, vulgarity and violence for their own sake.
Critics have repeatedly attacked him rather bitterly for his
descriptions of the Tommy; they have quibbled and wrangled
over the Kiplingesque coarseness of the slang and they have
held up their hands because he dares to give some barrack-
room reflections about women. 'I've 'ad my pickin' o'
sweet'earts, An' four o' the lot was prime,' says the Tommy in
'The Ladies' (1896), and the epitome of the poem is given in
the line, 'For the more you 'ave known o' the others/The less
will you settle to one.' (*DE* 442—3) As far as the charge of
violence is concerned, the poem 'Loot' (1890) is usually cited
as proof:

> (*Chorus*) Loo! loo! Lulu! lulu! Loo! loo! Loot! loot!
> loot!
> > Ow, the loot!
> > Bloomin' loot!
> > That's the thing to make the boys git up an'
> > shoot!
> > It's the same with dogs an' men,
> > If you'd make 'em come again
> > Clap 'em forward with a Loo! loo! Lulu! Loot!
> > Whoopee! Tear 'im, puppy! Loo! loo! Lulu!
> > Loot! loot! loot!
> >
> > (*DE* 410)

The sentiments expressed in these two poems are certainly deplorable. Yet while it is true that Kipling, akin to the Elizabethans in many ways, had a psychological interest in violence, one cannot attribute the vulgar sentiments of these poems to their writer. He is simply presenting the Tommy in all of his varied aspects — good and bad. He hides nothing, glosses over nothing. The above-mentioned poems only indicate that he is aware of the level to which a soldier can degenerate: it does not mean that he is advocating brutality, violence and anarchy. It would be ridiculous to accuse Kipling, the advocate of the Law, of championing Chaos and Disorder.

The dedication to *Barrack-Room Ballads* (1892) shows clearly why Kipling praises the soldier despite his vulgarity and coarseness. No matter what his faults may be the soldier, in Kipling's eyes, is an instrument for the enforcement of the Law. For Kipling military discipline is not merely a man-made expedient but a reflection of a larger order, namely the Law: hence his admiration for the soldier. The *Ballads* are dedicated to these unknown instruments of the Law: 'the Strong Men ranged thereby,/who had done his work and held his peace and had no fear to die,' and 'They know of toil and the end of toil; they know God's Law is plain'. (*DE* 84) It would appear from the dedicatory poem that their struggle against lawlessness and the Dark Forces does not end even in heaven, which is under constant attack from Evil:

> 'Tis theirs to sweep through the ringing deep where
>   Azrael's outposts are,
> Or buffet a path through the Pit's red wrath when
>   God goes out to war,
> Or hang with the reckless Seraphim on the rein of a
>   red-maned star.

> (*DE* 84)

'Danny Deever' (1890), the first poem in the *Ballads,* is worth noticing for the way it presents the crime of a soldier as an offence not only against the Queen's law or even the laws of civilised man, but against the Law of the universe of which he is a part. The ceremonial execution of Danny Deever seems to symbolise the ruthless rejection of one who is not man enough to keep the Law. It is interesting to note

that he lacks courage — ' "For 'e shot a comrade sleepin' —" '
and was ' "a sneakin' shootin' hound" '. (*DE* 397)

The universe has no place for a coward in Kipling's view,
although it must be stressed that Kipling would be the last
person to call a man a coward because he felt afraid. The
unpardonable sin is the kind of spiritual cowardice which
characterises Tomlinson, who is not man enough to enter
heaven or hell. At the behest of Satan the little devils go to
'husk this whimpering thief that comes in the guise of a man'
and they report:

> 'The soul that he got from God he has bartered clean away.
> 'We have threshed a stook of print and book, and
>   winnowed a chattering wind,
> 'And many a soul wherefrom he stole, but his we cannot
>   find.
> 'We have handled him, we have dandled him, we have
>   seared him to the bone,
> 'And, Sire, if tooth and nail show truth he has no soul of
>   his own.'
>
> (*DE* 364)

The devil is compassionate (as also in a later story 'Uncoven-
anted Mercies' (1932)) and sends him back to earth:

> 'Ye are neither spirit nor spirk,' he said; 'ye are neither
>   book nor brute —
> 'Go, get ye back to the flesh again for the sake of Man's
>   repute.'
>
> (*DE* 365)

The worst sins are not the conventional ones. What is
essential is to be positive: it is the indispensable basis of all
valuable actions. Kamal ('The Ballad of East and West') and
Abdur Rahman ('The Amir's Homily') are not exactly
worthy characters, and yet Kipling considers them in some
respects admirable because they are true to themselves.
Tomlinson and Danny Deever are the most unhappy souls
because they lack the courage to be men.

'A Conference of the Powers' (1890) provides a good indication of the basis for Kipling's admiration of the soldier. The
story presents three subalterns on leave from Asia who are

now assembled in London. Their role is not readily understood by the novelist Eustace Cleever, though the soldiers can appreciate his art. The Infant makes the novelist understand the kind of job the subalterns are doing by narrating the story of war in Upper Burma:

'The dacoits were having a first-class time, y'know —
filling women up with kerosine and setting 'em alight, and
burning villages, and crucifying people.'

The wonder in Eustace Cleever's eyes deepened. He
could not quite realise that the cross still existed in any
form.

'Have you ever seen a crucifixion?' said he.

'Of course not. 'Shouldn't have allowed it if I had; but
I've seen the corpses. . . .'

(3 575)

Maintenance of law and order is thus defined as one of the main tasks of the soldier. Futhermore Kipling is here concerned with the qualities of the soldiers who are involved in the enforcement of law and order more than with the enlargement of frontiers. A confrontation with the Dark Powers leads to a sharpening of the qualities of discipline, loyalty, courage, sense of duty and obedience, which are essential for the upholder of the Law. In *Stalky and Co.* (1899), for instance, frontier-soldiering becomes a ritual not so much for the sake of the Empire as for the qualities which these campaigns seem to inculcate in the Empire-builder.

The two cockney drummer boys in the well-known story 'The Drums of the Fore and Aft' (1888) display the above-mentioned qualities when their regiment is ready to break ranks and flee. Jakin and Lew are no supermen. The boys are about fourteen, and they drink, swear and fight viciously between themselves and against others. But an engagement with the enemy brings out their latent heroic qualities when the men of the Fore and Aft take to their heels. Two tried regiments on either flank — one Highland, the other Gurkha — look on in horror and indignation. And then, between this routed force and the advancing Afghans, Jakin and Lew appear, marching side by side and summoning their comrades to retrieve their honour. An Afghan volley soon drops both boys dead, and the story ends. Although no doubt the boys are slightly drunk, it is still their training and rigid discipline that make them perform their duty well:

> But some say, and among these be the Gurkhas who watched on the hillside, that that battle was won by Jakin and Lew, whose little bodies were borne up just in time to fit two gaps at the head of the big ditch-grave for the dead under the heights of Jagai.

(3 525–6)

The finest expression of a steady, unspectacular and even unrecognised performance of duty is seen in the character of a Gurkha soldier representing the Indian Armies at the King's funeral in London. Immobile, head bowed, choked by his high stiff collar, he keeps his place by the King's bier for three and a half hours (the British soldiers cannot endure even one hour), watching the endless procession of mourners' feet. The Gurkha acts out of a sense of personal integrity rather than a hope for recognition. This episode seems to imply that failure to do one's duty is more to be feared than either pain or death. This note of the drill-sergeant breathes in every line of Kipling's verse and prose, and in *Soldiers Three* (1888) he has done his best to revive a dying faith in discipline. Despite their roughness Privates Ortheris, Mulvaney and Learoyd are the best products of a sound drill-book training.

The most explicit statement by Kipling on the role of a soldier is contained in the story of Parnesius, included in *Puck of Pook's Hill* (1906). Parnesius, a Centurion of the Thirtieth Legion, is assigned the duty of defending the Wall against the onslaughts of the Picts and the Winged Hats. The Wall which separates civilisation from savagery is an obvious symbol of the Law. The Picts and the Winged Hats stand for the Dark Powers. The task of Parnesius is further complicated by the conflict between Maximus, Parnesius' General, and Theodosius: the defence of the Wall under these circumstances is almost beyond any hope. Yet Parnesius will stand guard no matter what happens: 'It concerns us to defend the Wall, no matter what Emperor dies or makes die.' (23 211)

3 *The Skilled Worker*

Kipling has been rightly hailed as the poet of modern machinery and technology. His work is so full of technical details about engines, bridges and microscopes that he has sometimes been ridiculed. 'The Ship that Found Herself' (1895) describes the maiden voyage of the *Dimbula,* a cargo-steamer of twelve hundred tons, of which her skipper says cautiously, 'I'm sayin' that it takes more than christenin' to mak' a ship. . . . She has to find herself yet.' So throughout the voyage from Liverpool to New York the different parts of the ship discuss their new experiences:

> 'It isn't distressingly calm now,' said the extra-strong frames — they were called web-frames — in the engine-room. 'There's an upward thrust that we don't understand, and there's a twist that is very bad for our brackets and diamond-plates, and there's a sort of west-north-westerly pull that follows the twist, which seriously annoys us. . . .'
> 'I'm afraid the matter is out of the owner's hands for the present,' said the Steam, slipping into the condenser.
> (13 103—4)

Engines and screws are most prominent in 'The Devil and the Deep Sea' (1895):

> The forward engine had no more work to do. Its released piston-rod, therefore, drove up fiercely, with nothing to check it, and started most of the nuts of the cylinder-cover. It came down again, the full weight of the steam behind it, and the foot of the disconnected connecting-rod, useless as the leg of a man with a sprained ankle, flung out to the right and struck the starboard, or right-hand, cast-iron supporting column of the forward engine, cracking it clean through about six inches above the base, and wedging the upper portion outwards three inches towards the ship's side. There the connecting-rod jammed. Meantime, the after-engine, being as yet unembarrassed, went on with its work, and in so doing brought round at its next revolution the crank of the forward engine, which smote the already jammed connecting-rod, bending it and therewith the

piston-rod cross-head — the big cross-piece that slides up and down so smoothly.

(13 186)

Kipling's rapture over modern technology does not, however, make him lose human interest; the man behind the machine is more important than the machine. Kipling revels in machinery because he sees the machine as an instrument which can be used for the advancement of the Law. This is skilfully suggested in the poem 'The Secret of the Machines' (1911) where the machines sing:

We can pull and haul and push and lift and drive,
We can print and plough and weave and heat and light,
We can run and race and swim and fly and dive,
We can see and hear and count and read and write!

(*DE* 729)

While it is a supreme song of the triumph of modern technology, the poem stresses the point that a proper use of the machine is essential for the progress of the Law; it is here that the importance of the man behind the machine becomes apparent:

But remember, please, the Law by which we live,
We are not built to comprehend a lie,
We can neither love not pity nor forgive.
If you make a slip in handling us you die!

(*DE* 730)

Among the men behind the machines Kipling is particularly full of praise for the engineer. Findlayson of 'The Bridge-Builders' deserves our admiration for the spirit of dedication with which he is doing construction work on the Ganges. 'McAndrew's Hymn' projects an ideal in the character of a Scottish marine engineer. Old McAndrew looks back on the progress he has made from the young days of debauchery to the time when he became a stern believer in his 'duty' and his 'work':

Obsairve! Per annum we'll have here two
        thousand souls abroad —
Think not I dare to justify myself before
        the Lord,

> But — average fifteen hunder souls safe-borne
>   fra' port to port —
> I *am* o' service to my kind. Ye wadna blame
>   the thought?
>   (*DE* 124)

His engines are the symbols of moral laws of the utmost
rigour for he is a Calvinist. They exact the same kind of duty
as his creed. And he goes on to talk of his beloved engines,
praises Robert Burns and sums up his philosophy of life in
these words:

> Lord, send a man like Robbie Burns to sing the
>   Song o' Steam!
> To match wi' Scotia's noblest speech yon orchestra
>   sublime
> Whaurto — uplifted like the Just— the tail-rods
>   mark the time.
> The crank-throws give the double-bass, the feed-pump
>   sobs an' heaves,
> An' now the main eccentrics start their quarrel on
>   the sheaves:
> Her time, her own appointed time, the rocking
>   link-head bides,
> Till — hear that note? — the rod's return whings
>   glimmerin' through the guides.
> They're all awa'! True beat, full power, the clangin'
>   chorus goes
> Clear to the tunnel where they sit, my purrin' dynamoes.
> Interdependence absolute, foreseen, ordained, decreed,
> To work, Ye'll note, at ony tilt an' every rate
>   o' speed.
> Fra' skylight-lift to furnace-bars, backed, bolted,
>   braced an' stayed,
> An' singin' like the Mornin' Stars for joy that they
>   are made;
> While, out o' touch o' vanity, the sweatin'
>   thrust-block says:
> 'Not unto us the praise, or man — not unto us the praise!'
> Now, a' together, hear them lift their lesson — theirs
>   an' mine:
> 'Law, Orrder, Duty an' Restraint, Obedience, Discipline!'
>   (*DE* 126)

We meet the engineers again in 'The Sons of Martha' (1907): they serve mankind to the best of their ability without any expectation of reward:

> It is their care in all the ages to take the buffet and
> cushion the shock.
> It is their care that the gear engages; it their care
> that the switches lock.
> It is their care that the wheels run truly; it is their
> care to embark and entrain,
> Tally, transport, and deliver duly the Sons of Mary by
> land and main.
>
> They say to mountains, 'Be ye removèd.' They say to
> the lesser floods, 'Be dry.'
> Under their rods are the rocks reprovèd — they are not
> afraid of that which is high.
> Then do the hill-tops shake to the summit — then is the
> bed of the deep laid bare,
> That the Sons of Mary may overcome it, pleasantly
> sleeping and unaware.
>
> $\hspace{8cm}$ (*DE* 382)

They undertake grave personal risks in the discharge of their duties:

> They finger death at their gloves' end where they piece
> and repiece the living wires.
> He rears against the gates they tend: they feed him
> hungry behind their fires.
> Early at dawn, ere men see clear, they stumble into his
> terrible stall,
> And hale him forth like a haltered steer, and goad and
> turn him till evenfall.
>
> $\hspace{8cm}$ (*DE* 383)

It is not for them to relax and enjoy: they are continuously busy in the glorious work:

> To these from birth is Belief forbidden; from these
> till death is Relief afar.
> They are concerned with matters hidden — under the
> earth-line their altars are —

The secret fountains to follow up, waters withdrawn
    to restore to the mouth,
And gather the floods as in a cup, and pour them
    again at a city's drouth.

                                 (DE 383)

They do not sit and pray to God for help as they know that
God helps those who help themselves:

They do not preach that their God will rouse them a
    little before the nuts work loose.
They do not teach that His Pity allows them to drop
    their job when they dam'-well choose.
As in the thronged and the lighted ways, so in the
    dark and the desert they stand,
Wary and watchful all their days that their brethern's
    days may be long in the land.

                                   (DE 383)

At times the engineer has to lay down his life in the discharge
of his duties and dies unnoticed and unsung:

Raise ye the stone or cleave the wood to make a path
    more fair or flat —
Lo, it is black already with blood some Son of Martha
    spilled for that!
Not as a ladder from earth to Heaven, not as a witness
    to any creed,
But simple service simply given to his own kind in
    their common need.

                                   (DE 383)

Besides the engineer Kipling is also full of praise for the
doctor. It is especially in his later career, when he was particularly concerned with the theme of healing, that the medical men figure in his work with great frequency. For example
we see the doctor at work in 'An Habitation Enforced'
(1905), 'A Doctor of Medicine' (1909), 'The Tender Achilles'
(1929) and 'Unprofessional' (1930). Speaking at the annual
dinner of the Royal College of Surgeons in February 1923
Kipling declared:

   '. . . He [the Surgeon] had more wonders beneath his knife
than earth or the planets had theretofore shown him. And

that was barely ten generations ago! Once again, the
Surgeon, as he had become, renewed his search, and once
again sacrificed himself in the search his passion drove him.
There is no anaesthesia so complete as man's absorption in
his own job.

(32 239—40)

4 The Peasant

The peasant does not appear very often in Kipling's works,
but whenever a reference is made to him one can immedi-
ately see the great respect and admiration in which he is held
by Kipling. In his Indian tales and verses it is the Indian
farmer who is treated with the greatest understanding and
veneration because he represents a fully-integrated society
which, however alien to the Western way of life, has its roots
in a civilisation as old as any in the world. His dislike of the
'university-trained hybrid' springs from an instinctive distrust
of the man who has deserted his own world for that of a
stranger, and has ended up belonging to neither. There are
many today who will agree that 'westernisation' is far from
an unmixed blessing; and Kipling, as his liking for things
genuinely Indian shows, tended to admire what was deep-
rooted in the soil of the country and nurtured over many
generations.

We have a glimpse of the Indian farmer, drawn with great
sensitivity, in a previously described story 'The Enlightenments of Pagett, M.P.' (1890). In a brief portrait of the Jat,
Kipling invests him with the simple, honest virtues of a man
of the earth. The poem 'The Masque of Plenty' (1888), mentioned in Chapter 4, brings out Kipling's deep concern for the
welfare of 'the sons of the soil'. His heart goes out to the
farmer who toils all his life and yet fails to get the returns
which should be his due:

> Our cattle reel beneath the yoke they bear —
>   The earth is iron, and the skies are brass —
> And faint with fervour of the flaming air
>   The languid hours pass.
>
> The well is dry beneath the village tree —
>   The young wheat withers ere it reach a span,
> And belts of blinding sand show cruelly
>   Where once the river ran.

(*DE* 36)

The Government contents itself, Kipling seems to say, with making superficial inquiries about the peasant without doing anything constructive to improve his lot; and the farmer's life remains a long-drawn question 'between a crop and a crop'.

Kipling's love of the country and the peasant is further seen in his settling in Sussex later in his life. In Kipling's time peasants and village craftsmen could still be found in Sussex; he studied them with great interest. He bought a small farm himself, which shows his love for the soil and for the tilling of the soil. Kipling had lived as a gypsy until the turn of the century when he began to feel himself rooted in the Sussex soil, and from then onwards the English landscape began to figure in his works. 'An Habitation Enforced' (1905) is a hymn to the healing power of the land which he himself experienced. The story tells of George Chapin and his wife Sophie who, after being broken by the sick hurry and divided aims of the materialistic American world, find health and peace in the quite and fruitful life of the English countryside. The regenerative powers of the soil are admirably brought out in 'A Charm' (1910), the opening piece in *Rewards and Fairies*. We are told to take a handful of English earth and lay it upon the heart:

> It shall sweeten and make whole
> Fevered breath and festered soul;
> It shall mightily restrain
> Over-busy hand and brain;
> It shall ease thy mortal strife
> 'Gainst the immortal woe of life,
> Till thyself restored shall prove
> By what grace the Heavens do move.
>
> (25 5)

It is understandable why Kipling admired a man rooted in the soil.

'Friendly Brook' (1914) is a purely pastoral tale. Hobden, the English peasant in 'The Land' — the poem that appears with the story — illustrates Kipling's respect for the cultivator. Through the story of Jim Wickenden and his gratitude to the brook that drowns his blackmailer, Kipling introduces us to a survival in the Sussex of his day of the animistic beliefs that are found in all primitive agricultural communities. And through the dialogue between Jim and another village labourer, who relate the story as they trim a neglected hedge, Kipling presents to us the self-respect, the inherited skill and the natural courtesy of the old countrymen of his day. 'Friendly Brook' brings out, in an indirect way, the sterling qualities of the peasantry — simplicity, humanity, toughness of character and a capacity to work hard.

C KIPLING'S IDEAL MAN – A BALANCE OF ACTION AND CONTEMPLATION

The foregoing section shows the type of man Kipling admired. He appears in numerous disguises — as a truly primitive Afghan fighter, an engineer aboard an ocean freighter, an English civil servant stationed in the outposts of the Empire, a doctor of medicine or even a Sussex farmer. He is certainly an example of the best in the group or the profession he represents, but he is no superman. He has his faults and shortcomings, but he commands our respect because of the following qualities:

1. He is a man of honour and strong character.
2. He knows his job in and out.
3. He is devoted to his job — his job assumes proportions larger than anything else in life.
4. He has a strong sense of responsibility and he performs his duty to the best of his ability in the most trying circumstances.
5. He is basically a man of action.
6. He is capable of love, suffering and self-sacrifice.

Kipling's emphasis on action, however, should not be taken to mean that he slights a life of contemplation. In fact, in Kipling's view, the ideal man is both a man of action and a man of contemplation. Kipling is too much of a realist not to know that Plato's ideal of a philosopher-king is not easy to translate into reality. Living the life of detached contemplation is given to very few, and the question remains whether such a life is laudable. Hence Kipling's message to the man in the street is an easily understandable one of positive action:

Heart may fail, and Strength outwear, and Purpose
    turn to Loathing,
But the everyday affair of business, meals, and clothing,
Builds a bulkead 'twixt Despair and the Edge of Nothing.

(DE 767)

Nevertheless Kipling does intimate the desirability of
following the golden mean by striking a balance between
action and contemplation, as we can see in 'The Miracle of
Purun Bhagat' (1894) and *Kim* (1901).

'The Miracle of Purun Bhagat' introduces us to Sir Purun
Dass, a highly educated and enlightened Prime Minister of a
native state in India. Under his administration schools,
colleges, hospitals and roads are built throughout the length
and breadth of the state. Consequently the Indian Government honours him with a knighthood, so that his name now
stands Sir Purun Dass, K.C.I.E.

However shortly thereafter Sir Purun Dass returns the
jewelled order of his knighthood to the Indian Government,
resigns position, palace and power, and takes up the begging
bowl and ochre-coloured dress of a *Sunnyasi* (holy man,
mystic). 'He had been, as the Old Law recommends,' Kipling
explains, 'twenty years a youth, twenty years a fighter, —
though he had never carried a weapon in his life, — and
twenty years head of a household . . . he had taken honour
when it came his way. . . . Now he would let those things go,
as a man drops the cloak he no longer needs'. (8 178)

Thus Purun Dass changes into Purun Bhagat and wanders
in search of 'his dream of peace and quiet'. Instinct leads him
to the Himalayas — the old symbol of spiritual achievement.
Beyond Simla Purun Bhagat discovers a deserted shrine on a
pass at an altitude of about twenty thousand feet. 'Here shall
I find peace,' says Purun to himself and enters into deep
meditation:

> That day saw the end of Purun Bhagat's wanderings. He
> had come to the place appointed for him — the silence and
> the space. After this, time stopped, and he, sitting at the
> mouth of the shrine, could not tell whether he were alive
> or dead; a man with control of his limbs, or a part of the
> hills, and the clouds, and the shifting rain and sunlight. He

would repeat a Name softly to himself a hundred times,
till, at each repetition, he seemed to move more and more
out of his body, sweeping to the doors of some tremen-
dous discovery; but, just as the door was opening, his body
would drag him back, and, with grief, he felt he was locked
up again in the flesh and bones of Purun Bhagat.

(8 184–5)

Purun Bhagat's renunciation of the world does not stop
him from loving mankind and other creatures of God. His
hermitage is open to all the animals of the Himalayas who
now become his constant companions. Purun Bhagat calls
them 'my brothers', and his low call of *'Bhai! Bhai!'* (brother,
brother) draws them from the forest at noon if they are
within earshot. The villagers in the valley come to know of
Purun Bhagat's presence at the shrine, and they revere him as
their patron saint.

Then the terrible rains come, and one night Bhagat realises
that the mountain is falling. There is no time to lose. He
rushes to the valley in order to warn the peasants of the
landslide. In doing so he loses his own life, but he saves the
villagers. This last act of Purun Bhagat makes him resume his
old role of Sir Purun Dass — a man of action — but there is
no indication whatsoever that the life of renunciation which
Purun chooses is unworthy. It is perhaps this new mystic
negative role that awakens Purun to a deeper understanding
of love, negative capability and capacity for self-sacrifice, and
leads him to act positively. The roles of a man of action and a
man of contemplation are fused together in a single personality. Thus Kipling seems to place a value on both ways of
life, and makes a plea for striking a balance between the two.

This theme comes out more sharply in *Kim*. There is no
doubt that although *Kim* has many features of an adventure
book for boys, with a teenager as its central figure, the novel
has a spiritual aspect as well which differentiates it from an
ordinary boy's tale. What sets *Kim* off from almost all the
other works of Kipling is that here Kipling probes the inner
personality of Kim, who is not merely a type as Kipling's
characters usually tend to be; he concerns himself with questions of self and identity. 'Who is Kim — Kim — Kim?' is the
crucial question that is posed by this novel.

The problem of determining his own identity is forced upon Kim's consciousness right from the beginning. Kim, of Irish parentage, has grown up as an orphan in the streets of Lahore. The half-caste woman who has looked after him tells him of his father's prophecy that he will know his own identity when he meets a red bull on a green field. Kim has no personal identity at this stage: he is 'The Little Friend of All the World'. Finding the open Indian street his natural habitation he is on intimate terms with policemen, beggars and grocers, and he can easily pass for a Hindu or a Muslim.

It is when Kim meets the Lama in front of the Zamzamah that he is first troubled with a quest for knowing himself. The Lama, he learns, has a quest of his own: he is in search of 'The River of the Arrow' that will bring him to *nirvana* — deliverance from the Wheel and total absorption in the Brahman. In other words the Lama is on a quest of total annihilation of the self and complete loss of identity, whereas Kim is in search of the self. Although Kim and the Lama have seemingly mutually exclusive goals before them, strangely enough they are bound together by the unbreakable *guru-chela* (master-disciple) relationship. ' "He has a search of his own," ' the Lama comments. ' "No river, but a Bull. Yea, a Red Bull on a green field will some day raise him to honour." ' However both the Lama and Kim repeatedly assert that they could not have gone on their quests without each other's help. The Lama continues to tell his audience that Kim ' "was sent of a sudden to aid me in this search, and his name is Friend of all the World," ' and he even contends that a bond existed between them in previous lives:

> Perhaps in a former life it was permitted that I should have rendered thee some service. May be (he smiled) I freed thee from a trap; or having caught thee on a hook in the days when I was not enlightened, cast thee back into the river again.
>
> (19 116)

Similarly Kim is so much attached to the old Lama that he would not leave him under any circumstances. At one stage in the novel he confesses that he has only two friends in the whole wide world — the Lama and Mahbub Ali.

Mahbub Ali, the Pathan horse-dealer of Lahore and a member of the Intelligence Service who loves the boy, presents another kind of world to him. The bustling Kashmiri Serai where the caravans from Central Asia unload their rich merchandise, the dancing girls of Lahore, the jingle of rupees and the Great Game of espionage are all parts of Mahbub's world: the masculine sphere of power, glamour and action. Kim is attracted to this world from the start but he is equally attracted by the serene world of the Lama, so from the very beginning he moves between the opposing worlds of Mahbub Ali and the Lama.

It is important to note that Kim does not identify himself completely with either Mahbub Ali or the Lama. He places a value on both action and detached contemplation: the Search and the Game exercise a double attraction for him. No choice is forced upon Kim; he goes through the novel with the Lama on the one hand and Mahbub Ali (with whom are soon associated Colonel Creighton, Lurgan and Hurree Babu) on the other. He understands the Game more readily than the Search, but the Lama's gentle, selfless wisdom is more compelling than the fascination of having a price on his head and a number instead of a name. These two worlds complement each other: the part in Kim which the Lama cannot satisfy gets its satisfaction in the activity of the Game.

Kim has therefore an ideal relationship with the Lama and Mahbub Ali. While the great Game makes him aware of the world of action, his spiritual and moral awakening is the direct result of the Lama's influence. From the playful boy that he is at the beginning he develops into a mature individual by the end of the novel. When the Lama asks if he wishes to leave him, Kim sternly replies, ' "No, I am not a dog or a snake to bite when I have learned to love." ' (19 444)

While it is true that Kim adopts a life of action by joining the secret service, in preference to the life of contemplation that the Lama represents, it should be noted that there is no real conflict in Kim's mind for the Lama himself approves of this choice. Kim, as Rao aptly observes, enters the 'great game' not merely as one who knows the rules, but as an individual with a deep understanding of the experience and meaning of life. To him, after his association with the Lama, the 'great game' becomes not merely a proper career for a sahib but one of responsibility, requiring human understanding. Indeed Kim rejects the least reference to his sahib-hood; what really matters is love, mutual help and affection. ' "Thou leanest on me in the body, Holy One, but I lean on thee for some other things," ' Kim confesses to the Lama. When Mahbub Ali tells the Lama of Kim's desire to join the 'great game', the Lama says:

> 'To that end he was prepared. I acquired merit in that I gave alms for his sake. A good deed does not die. He aided me in my Search. I aided him in his. Just is the Wheel, O horse-seller from the North. Let him be a teacher. Let him be a scribe. What matter? He will have attained Freedom at the end. The rest is illusion.'
>
> (19 446)

Kim has his master's complete approval in his new career.

So we see that the story of *Kim* is, in a way, a parable of self-knowledge. Kim begins his quest for knowledge of his own self; he learns that this goal can be achieved only by involvement in life; and since involvement must be purposeful it is the Lama who proves most helpful in defining the purpose. The Lama's message is one of love and humanity. Although he has renounced the world, at the very moment of his *nirvana* the Lama is concerned with love and human relationships, as is suggested by the creative images that Kipling uses to describe the Lama's release from the Wheel: 'As the egg from the fish, as the fish from the water, as the water from the cloud, as the cloud from the thick air; so put forth, so leaped out, so drew away, so fumed up the Soul of the Teshoo Lama from the Great Soul.' (19 472)

Kipling's ideal man is perhaps best suggested by the well-known poem 'If —', which appears along with the story 'Brother Square-Toes' (1910). 'If —', of the genre known as wisdom or 'gnomic' poetry, summarises the qualities of Kipling's ideal man[14] which belong to both the worlds of action and thought. The ideal man keeps a balance between these seemingly antithetical areas of human activity:

If you can dream — and not make dreams your master;
  If you can think — and not make thoughts your aim;
If you can meet with Triumph and Disaster
  And treat those two imposters just the same;
If you can bear to hear the truth you've spoken
  Twisted by knaves to make a trap for fools,
Or watch the things you gave your life to, broken,
  And stoop and build 'em up with worn-out tools:

If you can make one heap of all your winnings
  And risk it on one turn of pitch-and-toss,
And lose, and start again at your beginnings
  And never breathe a word about your loss;
If you can force your heart and nerve and sinew
  To serve your turn long after they are gone,
And so hold on when there is nothing in you
  Except the Will which says to them: 'Hold on!'

If you can talk with crowds and keep your virtue,
  Or walk with Kings — nor lose the common touch,
If neither foes nor loving friends can hurt you,
  If all men count with you, but none too much;
If you can fill the unforgiving minute
  With sixty seconds' worth of distance run,
Yours is the Earth and everything that's in it,
  And — which is more — *you'll be a Man,* my son!

(DE 577. Italics mine.)

6 Education in the Law in Four Children's Books

As the creeper that girdles the tree-trunk the Law runneth
forward and back —
For the strength of the Pack is the Wolf, and the strength of
the Wolf is the Pack.

'The Law of the Jungle', *DE* 558

A BACKGROUND: CHILDREN'S BOOKS AS EDUCATIONAL MANUALS

In the foregoing chapters I have presented three interrelated aspects of Kipling's Law: moral values, the Imperial Idea and the Doctrine of Action. This master idea of Law is most fully expounded in four children's books — *The Jungle Book* (1894), *The Second Jungle Book* (1895), *Puck of Pook's Hill* (1906) and *Rewards and Fairies* (1910). *The Jungle Books* are concerned mainly with the exposition of moral values and the Doctrine of Action, the Puck books with the Power of History and the Imperial Idea in particular.

The Jungle Books and the Puck books, while primarily children's books, are secondarily educational manuals and thirdly a mixture of unsustained allegory, fable, myth, history and romance. The continual shift of perspective in these tales complicates the task of analysing them, but the main outlines of what Kipling is doing are very clear to see. Here Kipling is a teacher of young children, didactic as well as entertaining, getting across a message in every case in the tradition of a series of school lessons through stories or parables or *exempla*. For the purpose of this study it is convenient to consider these children's books as educational manuals.

Kipling was quite familiar with the long tradition behind children's literature; he particularly displays a deep knowledge of some of the prominent Victorian writers for children — especially Lewis Carroll, Robert Louis Stevenson and H. Rider Haggard. In his childhood Kipling had absorbed *Alice's*

Adventures in Wonderland (1865) so completely that it was as much a part of him as the Bible or the Prayer Book. Haggard became his personal friend, and a phrase from Haggard's *Nada the Lily* (1892) helped crystalize his idea for the Mowgli stories. (36 110) He also read Mrs Ewing and E. Nesbit with great interest. Among the writers of tales for boys he was particularly familiar with Ainsworth, Henty, Ballantyne and Dean Farrar.[1]

Yet the Jungle and Puck books are not limited to children; they are meant for adults as well. It would be a shallow criticism of *The Jungle Books* to call them animal stories for children, though that is the way in which they first enthral readers. Like their great original, *Aesop's Fables,* or like the *Jatakas,* which the Kiplings knew so well, they impress themselves on the mind at more than one level. Sir Philip Sidney's reference in his *Defence of Poesy* to 'a tale which holdeth children from play and old men from the chimney corner'[2] may well be applied to both *The Jungle Books* and the Puck books.

B THE LAW AND SOCIAL ORDER IN
THE JUNGLE BOOKS

An exposition of the nature of the Law is one of Kipling's main aims in *The Jungle Books* in general and the Mowgli stories in particular. One of the first few words that one hears in these stories is Law: 'Oh, hear the call! — Good hunting all/That keep the Jungle Law!' ('Night-Song in the Jungle' with which the collection opens). And the word Law runs like a leitmotiv through the entire volume.

The scene of most of the Jungle stories is laid in the Indian Jungle on the bank of Waingunga. The Jungle, symbolic of the world, is governed by the Law of the Jungle, which is 'by far the oldest law in the world' (7 77); but this Law must not be confused with lawlessness as it has 'arranged for almost every kind of accident that may befall the Jungle People, till now its code is as perfect as time and custom can make it . . . and it was Baloo who told him [Mowgli] . . . that the Law was like the Giant Creeper, because it dropped across every one's back and no one could escape'. (7 77) This explains why Kipling refers to the Law, however perfect, as the

Law of the Jungle and not of the Garden. Being a realist he knows that the Jungle (i.e. the world) can only tend towards the Garden, that the law of this world can only be 'as perfect as time and custom can make it'. From this it follows that the Jungle Law is meant to be a practical code rather than a utopian dream that can never be realised.

The Law of the Jungle is presented as a principle of order which has emerged out of lawlessness — one of the main sources of primitive law often generated in disorder and dispute. Law determines which course of action posed by the disputants will be allowed to prevail and which will be suppressed by legal authority. Rules of law, emerging from a dispute, rest on deep-lying assumptions concerning the nature of the universe and man and of what is desirable and undesirable.

Kipling hints at this source of the Law in the tale narrated by Hathi on the day of the water-truce. This myth takes us back to the paradisal state (before the Fall) when all the animals lived in perfect harmony in the Jungle under the benevolent eyes of the god Tha, the First of the Elephants. Then Evil entered the Jungle and things changed. The flowers and fruits and trees withered away, the river Waingunga dried up and the animals began to fight among themselves over food. The god Tha was disturbed by this onslaught of Evil, but he was too 'busy making new jungles and leading the rivers in their beds' to intervene personally in order to set things right in the old Jungle. Tha, however, appointed the First of the Tigers as his deputy and entrusted him with the task of maintaining peace in the Jungle.

One night there was a minor dispute between two bucks and they came to the Tiger for a settlement. The Tiger, forgetting that he was the deputy of Tha and the judge of the Jungle, leaped upon one of the bucks and broke his neck. This was the first time that Death entered the Jungle. Seeing what he had done the Tiger fled to the Marshes of the North, and the Jungle was left without a master. Consequently a period of chaos returned and all the animals fell to fighting among themselves. On hearing the noise Tha came down and asked: 'Who will now be master of the Jungle People?' The Ape volunteered himself for the job but he had no understanding of Tha's purpose: he only brought further confusion to the Jungle. The god Tha could not tolerate any more disorder and chaos so he created a comprehensive Law for the maintenance of harmony in the Jungle, telling the animals in a firm voice:

> 'The first of your masters has brought Death into the Jungle, and the second Shame. Now it is time there was a Law, and a Law that ye must not break.'

> (7 94)

The parallel between Hathi's narrative and the story of the Garden in Genesis is quite striking. Hathi's story makes us see God as the source of all law; the Law of the Jungle therefore assumes the proportions of divine positive law — the law given by God to man in addition to the natural law.

The Law of the Jungle is based on five essential elements: (i) Reason, (ii) the Common Good, (iii) Ethical Values, (iv) Law-making Authority and Promulgation, (v) Custom and Tradition.

Reason. Since law is a rule and measure whereby man is induced to act or refrain from acting, it is evidently a product of practical reason. The will of the competent authority must also be present to set the lawmaking process in motion; but what is made must accord with some rule of reason to have the nature of the law. The will of the sovereign, for example, is the efficient cause of the law, while reason is its formal cause. Reason is intrinsic to Law; will, however necessary genetically, remains none the less an extrinsic factor. Hence the most important feature of the Law of the Jungle is that it is rational, it is the antithesis of *dewanee* (Urdu for 'madness', 'irrationality') of which all the Jungle People are afraid as it is 'the most disgraceful thing that can overtake a wild creature'. (7 2) The rational basis of the law is further shown by the reason why the Law of the Jungle forbids the killing of Man:

> The Law of the Jungle, which never orders anything without a reason, forbids every beast to eat Man. . . . The real reason for this is that man-killing means, sooner or later, the arrival of white men on elephants, with guns, and

hundreds of brown men with gongs and rockets and torches. Then everybody in the Jungle suffers.

(7 4—5)

It is obviously the common sense reason of self-preservation which is behind the clause that forbids man-killing.

Common Good. The common good is the final cause of law. In the case of eternal law, this is the good of the whole creation under the governance of divine providence. In the case of natural law, the common fountainhead of ethics and jurisprudence, it is man's ultimate happiness, which consists in the perfection of the human person, and mutual friendship between man and man. In the case of human law, it is the well-being of the people and the public welfare of the political community.

The Law of the Jungle is geared to the attainment of common good: '... the strength of the Pack is the Wolf, and the strength of the Wolf is the Pack.' (*DE* 558) The rules of conduct stipulated by the Code of the Seeonee Wolf Pack underline the importance of the common good as the informing principle of the Law. For example, the Code strictly forbids needless warfare as it may weaken the community. ' "You will remember," ' Mowgli tells the quarreling wolves in 'The Spring Running', ' "that the Law of the Jungle forbids fighting where the Pack can see" '. (7 270) Similarly in the poem 'The Law of the Jungle', which accompanies the story 'How Fear Came', we are told:

When Pack meets with Pack in the Jungle, and neither will
    go from the trail,
Lie down till the leaders have spoken — it may be fair
    words shall prevail.

When ye fight with a Wolf of the Pack, ye must fight him
    alone and afar,
Lest others take part in the quarrel, and the Pack be
    diminished by war.

(*DE* 558—9)

However in case of danger to the community the Law prescribes immediate offensive action in order to protect the

society from disintegration. This message of positive action
for common good is particularly illustrated in 'Kaa's Hunting', 'Red Dog', and 'Rikki-Tikki-Tavi'. In 'Kaa's Hunting' the
monkeys, the people 'without the Law', intrude in the
Jungle, and the followers of the Law take immediate action
against them. In 'Red Dog' the Jungle is invaded by the
ferocious red Deccan dogs. On the advice of Mowgli and
Akela the pack decides to fight rather than surrender to the
enemy, and ultimately the forces of disorder are defeated.
Similarly the young mongoose Rikki in the story 'Rikki-
Tikki-Tavi' undertakes grave personal risk in fighting against
the cobras, symbols of lawlessness, in order to restore the
peace and harmony of the entire community.

Ethical Values.　　Since Plato and Aristotle most of the disputes about the meaning of law have also been disputes about
the nature of both law and morality and about the relation of
the two. The fact that ethics and law are both concerned
with conduct, and refer to the natural law in formulating
directions, has led to much confusion in jurisprudence.
Theories of the relationship extend from those which hold
that law should implement ethical decisions by force to those
which hold that law is entirely unrelated to ethics. A sharp
distinction between law and morality is, in fact, neither
possible nor desirable. The end of both law and ethics is to
make man good, teaching him to practise virtue and refrain
from vice. But ethics impels man through an internal
principle, while law impels man through an external principle.
principle.

The Law of the Jungle is firmly based on moral and ethical
values. This is amply borne out by its code of private and
public conduct. Here are a few examples:

1. Moderation: '. . . drink deeply, but never too deep;/And
   remember the night is for hunting, and forget not the day
   is for sleep.' (*DE* 558)
2. Respect for elders: 'Keep peace with the Lords of the
   Jungle — the Tiger, the Panther, the Bear;/And trouble not
   Hathi the Silent, and mock not the Boar in his lair.' (*DE*
   558)
3. Kindness to both young and old: The Law forbids attack

on the young cubs until they have killed their first buck. (7 12) Similarly Baloo teaches Mowgli to take care of Akela in his old age. (7 145)

4. Fortitude: as exhibited by Father Wolf when Shere Khan the Tiger demands the return of Mowgli: ' "The Wolves are a free people. They take orders from the Head of the Pack, and not from any striped cattle-killer. The man's cub is ours — to kill if we choose," ' he tells the tiger. (7 7)

5. The Value of One's Word: At the time of the attack of the red Deccan dogs, Mowgli tells Kaa of his determination to fight the dholes along with the wolf pack — the Free People. ' "Free People," ' Kaa grunts, ' ". . . And thou hast tied thyself into the death-knot for the sake of the memory of dead wolves! This is no good hunting." ' Mowgli remains firm: ' "It is my word which I have spoken. The trees know, the river knows. Till the dholes have gone by my word comes not back to me." ' And Kaa has to agree with him: ' "*Ngssh*! That changes all trails. I had thought to take thee away with me to the northern marshes, but the word — even the word of a little, naked, hairless manling — is a word." ' (7 230)

6. The danger of Pride and the need for Humility: 'If ye plunder his Kill from a weaker, devour not all in thy pride;/Pack-Right is the right of the meanest. . . .' (*DE* 559) Bagheera advises Mowgli: 'Make no *bandar's* boast of skill;/Hold thy peace above the kill.' (7 294)

7. Devotion to vocation or work: 'Let nor call nor song nor sign/Turn thee from thy hunting-line.' (7 294) The same lesson is conveyed in 'Quiqern', a story of the North, in which Kotuko, an Eskimo boy, and his dog save the whole community from starvation by their heroism and devotion to work.

There are two values — namely love and justice — strongly advocated by *The Jungle Books,* which are not explicitly set forth in any clause of the code of the Seeonee Wolf Pack.

The importance of love in the code of values followed by the Jungle People is amply exhibited in the relationship between Mowgli and the animals. Love as an action of sacrifice may be seen in the way the animals and Mowgli put them-

selves in great danger for each other's sake. Baloo, Bagheera
and Kaa undertake grave risks to rescue Mowgli from the
clutches of the *Bandar-log*. On Mowgli's return to the Jungle
after his maltreatment at the hands of the villagers, the possibility of Mowgli's pursuit by the Man-Pack is considered by
the animals, and the Wolf Brothers prove their love for
Mowgli by stressing that they would sacrifice their lives for
his sake. Mowgli has similar feelings for the animals of the
Jungle: when the red dogs attack he decides to stay with the
pack though he could have easily escaped from the Jungle with
Kaa.

Love as an emotion of grief at loss is amply illustrated by
the jungle stories. At the time of Mowgli's departure from the
Jungle, the animals lament:

> Man goes to Man! Cry the challenge through the Jungle!
>   He that was our Brother goes away.
> Hear, now, and judge, O ye People of the Jungle, —
>   Answer, who shall turn him — who shall stay?
>
> Man goes to Man! He is weeping in the Jungle:
>   He that was our Brother sorrows sore!
> Man goes to Man! (Oh, we loved him in the Jungle!)
>   To the Man-Trail where we may not follow more.
>
> (7 260)

And Gray-Brother speaks in highly moving words:

> 'Man-cub — Master of the Jungle — Son of Raksha, Lair-
> brother to me — though I forget for a little while in the
> spring, thy trail is my trail, thy lair is my lair, thy kill is my
> kill, and thy death-fight is my death-fight. I speak for the
> Three.'
>
> (7 288)

The scene of Mowgli's final leave-taking from the Jungle
People is charged with emotion. ' "*Hai-mai*, my brothers,"
cried Mowgli, throwing up his arms with a sob. "I know not
what I know! I would not go; but I am drawn by both feet.
How shall I leave these nights?" ' (7 291) But having cast the
skin he cannot creep into it afresh. ' "It is hard to cast the
skin," ' says Kaa as Mowgli 'sobbed and sobbed, with his

head on the blind bear's side and his arms around his neck, while Baloo tried feebly to lick his feet'. (7 292) Love thus creates the bond between the animals and Mowgli which is a prerequisite for the establishment of an ideal tribal (and hence social) structure.

The importance of justice is set forth in many episodes in *The Jungle Books*. For instance after Mowgli's expulsion from the village, Messua and her husband, who adopted Mowgli and called him Nathoo after their dead son, are to be burnt at the stake for witchcraft; so they decide to go to the town of Khanhiwara to seek justice. ' "If we reach Khanhiwara, and I get the ear of the English," ' says Messua's husband, ' "I will bring such a law-suit against the Brahmin and old Buldeo and the others as shall eat this village to the bone. They shall pay me twice over for my crops untilled and my buffaloes unfed. I will have a great justice." ' (7 162) Though Mowgli has never heard the word 'justice', he has his own notion of it: ' "I do not know what justice is, but — come thou back next rains and see what is left," ' he replies. And a short time afterwards the beasts and especially elephants invade the village; they raze it to the ground as a vengeance against the villagers' mistreatment of Mowgli, Messua and her husband. In a later story we are told that the execution of rough justice on the village made Mowgli feel good: 'He had the good conscience that comes from paying a just debt.' (7 219) Further on we are briefly told how, breaking his knife on the back-plates of a vicious crocodile, he finds a new and longer knife round the neck of a man who had been killed by a wild boar. He tracks that boar and kills him as a just and fair price for the knife.

The concept of justice in the Jungle stories may appear close to revenge, but this need not trouble the reader too much. One should remember that these stories are set in a primitive society where revenge is certainly one form of justice. In the *Just So Stories* (1902), moreover, we do see 'just deserts' or 'just rewards' in how things came to be as we know them — the elephant's trunk, the camel's hump, the whale's throat and so forth.

Again it should be noted that justice, like love, is essential for an ideal social order.

Law-making Authority and Promulgation.   Authority is the efficient cause of law. The very existence of law implies the existence of a law-maker. God is the sole author of the eternal law, as also of the natural law, which He has ingrained in man's nature. All systems of human law thus contain, in varying proportions, a natural law element and a positive law element. The former is not made by man but only declared by him, whereas the latter is man-made.

The story of the coming of the Law, as narrated by Hathi, indicates that the Law of the Jungle has the authority of God behind it (see pages 123—4 above). This law is, however, not simply the divine law or natural law; it also includes elements of man-made or positive law. This aspect of the Law of the Jungle is shown by the provision which allows the leader of the pack to make new rules and regulations for a situation not already dealt with by the Law: 'Because of his age and his cunning, because of his gripe and his paw,/ In all that the Law leaveth open, the word of the Head Wolf is Law.' (*DE* 560) The Law cannot function without the authority of the leader. Thus in 'Tiger! Tiger!' we see that the Free People have grown lawless for the lack of a leader. ' "Lead us again, O Akela," ' the wolves howl, ' "Lead us again, O Man-cub, for we be sick of this lawlessness, and we would be the Free People once more." ' (7 134)

Promulgation and enforcement constitute the material cause of law. The Law of the Jungle is enforced by the council of wolves. The form of command in which the Law is couched gives us an idea of the force with which it is promulgated: '*Now these are the Laws of the Jungle, and many and mighty are they;/But the head and the hoof of the Law and the haunch and the hump is — Obey!*' (*DE* 560)

Custom and Tradition.   Law is generically similar to custom in that it also prescribes patterns of behaviour. It is a characteristic of human social life that what is done by the majority in a given situation takes on the quality of what ought to be done. The norm takes on the quality of the normative. The inclusion of custom and tradition in the Law of the Jungle may be seen in the practice that if there is any dispute as to the right of a cub to be accepted by the Pack, he must be spoken for by at least two members of the Pack who are not related to him. (7 11) Similarly the law stipulating that no animal has the right to change his quarters without due warning is based on custom. (7 3)

The Law of the Jungle is thus an instrument of establishing a harmonious social order. One of the fundamental questions with which Kipling seems to be preoccupied, as Noel Annan points out, is: 'What holds society (or an organisation) together?'³ And Kipling finds the answer in religion, custom and convention, morality, law — the forces of social control — which impose upon individuals certain rules which they break at their peril.

C PSYCHOLOGICAL ALLEGORY IN
THE JUNGLE BOOKS

The Jungle Books are concerned not only with a study of order on the social level but also with order on the individual level. The fables of *The Jungle Books* have both social and psychological implications, though of course it may be admitted that the social aspect of *The Jungle Books,* as suggested in the preceding section, is of primary importance. Kipling's sense of the importance of society has, none the less, been too heavily stressed; for however much he felt that man should give himself to something greater than himself and lose himself in the giving, he felt also that man hankers after being himself — which perhaps he can be only after the giving.

Before analysing the psychological allegory of *The Jungle Books* (in particular the Mowgli stories) it would be helpful to note that often the allegorical hero — or rather the conceptual hero — is not so much a real person as a generator of secondary personalities, which are partial aspects of himself. These agents stand for abstract ideas and they give a sort of life to intellectual conceptions. Through this technique the writer is able to project clearly what goes on in the mind of the protagonist. It would therefore appear that the Mowgli fables are concerned with a single person, that is, Mowgli. But Mowgli himself is not an individual: the shadow of Adam looms heavily on him. He is actually referred to as Adam by the German forest officer in 'In the Rukh':

'Dis man haf lived, and he is an anachronism, for he is before der Iron Age, and der Stone Age. Look here, he is at der beginnings of der history of man — Adam in der Garden, und now we want only an Eva!'

(7 331–2)

Mowgli may therefore be taken to stand for the generic Man.

Apart from Mowgli the main characters in the Jungle fables are animals through whom different aspects of Mowgli's personality are projected. We may note that it is only appropriate for Kipling to introduce beasts into these tales because (a) his medium of fable usually requires beasts and (b) animals are eminently suited for the personification of an abstract idea or a human trait as they can be easily associated with a single characteristic. Moreover one should also bear in mind that these fables are set in India where animals are frequently employed as symbols in religious iconographies. Let us now take a look at the beast symbolism in *The Jungle Books.*

Shere Khan, the lame tiger, represents the brute animal power which defies all restraints. The Bandar-log, or monkeys, symbolise lawlessness, flattery, lasciviousness and maliciousness. Tabaqui, the jackal, is an objectification of one's desire to lead the life of a parasite. Considered as a whole, Shere Khan, Bandar-log and Tabaqui stand for the Dark Powers that reside within one's heart.

Another group of animals represents the positive side of Man's mind. The wolves symbolise tenacity and firmness. Baloo, the bear, is an objectification of endurance and experience. Bagheera, the panther, is bravery, might and swiftness of action. Hathi, the elephant, is a well-known symbol of intellect and wisdom. (In Hindu mythology the elephant is an aspect of Ganesha, the god of wisdom.) Kaa, the python, stands for intelligence, prudence and perhaps memory. (The Hindu *naga* symbolises every branch of learning.)

The symbolic action of these stories thus concerns the inner conflict between the forces of Order and Disorder, or Good and Evil, that goes on in the mind of Mowgli. This symbolic action falls into two well-known patterns, which may be labelled *battle* and *progress*.

The allegorical progress may first of all be understood in the narrow sense of a questing journey, for example Christian's journey to the Celestial City in *Pilgrim's Progress*. The progress need not, however, involve a physical journey. The whole operation can be presented as a sort of introspective journey through the self: Kafka's 'The Burrow' with its ruminations for instance. This progress is always marked by an internal conflict of ideas and ideals, whose figurative base is nevertheless a technological military one. It is therefore usually described as an actual conflict on a field of battle. Progress and battle in Kipling present an orderly or definite sequence of events which are often ritualised. The sequence of repeated elements is a kind of symbolic *dance,* to use Kenneth Burke's word.[4]

With this framework in mind let us direct our attention to *battle* and *progress* in the fables of *The Jungle Books*. 'Kaa's Hunting' is the best example of the recurrent battle that goes on within Mowgli's mind between the Forces of Order and Disorder, Law and Lawlessness and Light and Darkness. At the beginning of this story we see Mowgli leaning towards the evil within him, when the voice of experience (Baloo) admonishes him: ' "Thou hast been with the Monkey-People — the gray apes — the people without a Law — the eaters of everything. That is great shame." ' (7 38) The dark side of Mowgli's mind tries to rationalise his bent towards the Forces of Lawlessness:

> 'When Baloo hurt my head,' said Mowgli, 'I went away, and the gray apes came down from the trees and had pity on me. No one else cared. . . . And then, and then, they gave me nuts and pleasant things to eat, and they — they carried me in their arms up to the top of the trees and said I was their blood-brother except that I had no tail, and should be their leader some day.'
>
> (7 40)

Temptation is soon followed by seduction. Mowgli disregards the advice of experience and reason (Baloo), and he lets himself be abducted by the Bandar-log, representing lawlessness. His journey on the green roads through the trees along which the monkeys take him to their city is an excellent objectification of Mowgli's state of mind:

> Two of the strongest monkeys caught Mowgli under the arms and swung off with him through the tree-tops, twenty feet at a bound. Had they been alone they could have gone twice as fast, but the boy's weight held them back. Sick and giddy as Mowgli was he could not help enjoying the wild rush, though the glimpses of earth far down below frightened him, and the terrible check and jerk at the end of the swing over nothing but empty air brought his heart between his teeth. . . . So, bounding and crashing and whooping and yelling, the whole tribe of *Bandar-log* swept along the tree-tops with Mowgli their prisoner.
> (7 44—5)

'Sick and giddy' Mowgli being swept along the tree-tops conjures up the topsy-turvey state of his mind at this point. His arrival in Cold Lairs, the city of the Bandar-log, reflects his surrender to the anarchy, disorder and lawlessness within him.

> Some king had built it [Cold Lairs] long ago on a little hill. You could still trace the stone causeways that led up to the ruined gates where the last splinters of wood hung to the worn, rusted hinges. Trees had grown into and out of the walls; the battlements were tumbled down and decayed, and wild creepers hung out of the windows of the towers on the walls in bushy hanging clumps. . . . From the palace you could see the rows and rows of roofless houses that made up the city looking like empty honeycombs filled with blackness.
> (7 56—7)

Cold Lairs is aptly projected as a city in ruins. Images of death, decay and darkness dominate this passage: 'ruined gates', 'decayed splinters of wood', 'rusted hinges', 'trees grown into and out of the walls', 'decayed battlements', 'roofless houses' and 'the city looking like empty honeycombs filled with blackness' build up images of the disease, barrenness and degeneration which characterise Mowgli's present state of mind.

All is not lost. Mowgli can still think, and the moment he does so he realises the mistake he has committed. While being dragged by the monkeys he sees Chil, the kite, who symbolises thinking; he asks her to inform Baloo of his plight: ' "Mark my trail. Tell Baloo of the Seeonee Pack and Bagheera of the Council Rock." ' (7 46)

After Mowgli's realisation of his mistake the Forces of Good gain strength. They muster their ranks and resolve to fight against the Dark Powers with renewed energy. ' "Haste! Oh haste! We may catch them yet!" ' Baloo, the voice of experience, tells others. Baloo and Bagheera are now more cautious in their estimation of the power of evil, so they seek advice and help of Kaa, the symbol of memory. The encounter between Baloo, Bagheera and Kaa is a good objectification of what goes on in one's mind when one rakes the memory for advice:

> They found him stretched out on a warm ledge in the afternoon sun, admiring his beautiful coat . . . darting his big blunt-nosed head along the ground, and twisting the thirty feet of his body into fantastic knots and curves. . . . Kaa was not a poison-snake. . . . his strength lay in his hug, and when he had once lapped his huge coils round anybody there was no more to be said. 'Good hunting!' cried Baloo, sitting on his haunches. Like all snakes of his breed, Kaa was rather deaf, and did not hear the call at first. Then he curled up ready for any accident, his head lowered.
>
> (7 49)

The turns, twists and coils of Kaa suggest the storehouse of past memories and experiences. Kaa's deafness, his slight indifference to Baloo at first and then his alertness indicate the various stages in which memory works.

The Good Powers in Mowgli finally prepare themselves for a decisive battle against the Evil Powers within him, as we see through the great battle that takes place in Cold Lairs between Bandar-log and Baloo, Bagheera and Kaa. Bandar-log, the forces of lawlessness, are vanquished, and Mowgli emerges as a better man with self-control and inner harmony. This is the *progress* that follows the *battle* in Cold Lairs.

The pattern of *battle* and *progress* recurs in several fables.

It may be noted that in each conflict Mowgli makes use of the experience gained in the previous one; thus his struggles represent the cumulative progress that is made by him. The victory in 'Kaa's Hunting' yields rich dividends in 'Tiger! Tiger!'. Here Mowgli is able to gain control over the evil within him with less difficulty, shown by the relative ease with which he kills Shere Khan, symbol of corrupt power. The next significant battle takes place in 'Red Dog' when the Forces of Disorder and Lawlessness make a last ditch struggle to subjugate Mowgli. These powers now appear in the shape of the ferocious red Deccan dogs — the people without the law. On hearing the news of the dogs' intrusion in the Jungle Mowgli, because of the progress that he has made in the previous battles, loses no time in preparing for the fight. And ultimately the powerful enemy is vanquished.

The final achievement of Mowgli may be seen in his progress from a Man-cub to a Master of the Jungle — from the days when he was a prey to passions, disorder and lawlessness to the acquiring of control over the jungle of passions and becoming a man with inner harmony. Mowgli's awareness of this progress is shown when Baloo, the old teacher of the Law, has to acknowledge Mowgli's great achievement: ' "Master of the Jungle, the Jungle is thine at call." ' ' "The Middle Jungle is thine also," ' says Kaa. (7 290) ' "Good hunting on a new trail, Master of the Jungle! Remember, Bagheera loved thee," ' adds Bagheera.(7 292)

This psychological allegory in *The Jungle Books*, however intermittent, indicates that Kipling was not blind to what goes on within the self in its struggle to realise itself, though it may be conceded that a probe into the human psyche was not his main concern.

D THE POWER OF HISTORY IN THE PUCK BOOKS

In the Puck books, Kipling explores the dimension of time as in his previous days he explored the dimension of space. He now sees the Law in relation to history — England's history in particular — and he binds the past and present together in an almost magical way. It is therefore not surprising to see that the real hero of these delightful tales is old Hobden, the farmer who carries the whole history and spirit of the valley in his bones.

In *Puck of Pook's Hill* and *Rewards and Fairies* historical evolution is fairly obvious though the events are described neither chronologically nor accurately. The important point to note, however, is that Kipling's interest in history is not that of a scholar but that of an imaginative writer. He deliberately takes many liberties with facts, dates and places, for his purpose is to appeal to the reader's imagination and present the whole pageant of English history from Anglo-Saxon days to Tudor times in particular. And he admirably succeeds in his aim. G. M. Trevelyan, one of the greatest historians of this age, pays rich tribute to the Puck stories for their vivid reflection of the spirit of their times:

> He tells us tale after tale of the ancient history of England, as he imagines it, with a marvellous historical sense, I think. The language and psychology of Romans, Saxons and Normans is frankly modern — 'subalterns again', if you like — but as no one knows how the people of those far-gone ages thought or spoke, there is no good using 'tushery', and Kipling's way of making them talk is as good as another. But we know a good deal about the historical and social surroundings in which they moved, and these Kipling has carefully studied and reproduced. Above all, the tales are alive and they are beautiful.[5]

The Power of History in the Puck books is conveyed in several subthemes expressive of the Law. The most important of these themes is the Imperial Idea which receives particular attention in *Puck of Pook's Hill.*

'Weland's Sword' introduces us to a magic sword bearing runes of prophecy, which is made by Weland, smith to the gods. Part of the inscription on the Sword runs as follows:

> *To gather Gold*
> *At the world's end*
> *I am sent.*
>
> *The Gold I gather*
> *Comes into England*
> *Out of deep Water.*

Like a shining Fish
Then it descends
Into deep Water.

It is not given
For goods or gear,
But for The Thing.
(23 133)

The Sword thus carries a divine purpose — 'The Thing'. The gathering of Gold is described as a step that leads to the achievement of the Thing.

After making the Sword, Weland presents it to Hugh the Saxon. In 'Young Men at the Manor' the Sword is given by Hugh to Sir Richard the Norman, and then Hugh receives it back before the journey South with Witta the Northman in 'The Knights of the Joyous Venture'. The Sword enables Hugh to fight the 'dragon' who guards the treasure on the African shore. The treasure is captured and finally brought over to England. The Sword thus serves part of its purpose by bringing the Gold. Later on in the story 'The Treasure and the Law' (1906) we see Gold leading to the birth of the Thing or the Law. This process is illustrated by the way in which Kadmiel the Jew makes King John sign Magna Carta on the promise of supplying the Gold that the King needs for his campaigns against France.

The Sword may well be a symbol of the Imperial Idea, which leads to the establishment of the Empire and possession of Gold. The next step in this process of evolution is the promulgation of the Thing or the Law. The symbolism of Sword and Thing is easily understandable, but the function of Gold presents certain difficulties which bring out the inconsistency of the allegory in *Puck of Pook's Hill*. Although Gold is described as a definite part of the purpose of the Sword, it is destroyed by Hugh, Sir Richard, De Aquila and Kadmiel. 'Gold changes men altogether' (23 93) and 'There can be no war without gold', (23 289) we are told in these tales. Nevertheless, the birth of the Law is said to be directly related to the gathering of Gold. Puck sums up the series: 'Weland gave the Sword! The Sword gave the Treasure, and the Treasure gave the Law. It is as natural as an oak growing.'

(23 301) The Law is presented here as more mysterious than it has seemed to be so far.[6]

In the Roman stories, however, Kipling makes a more explicit statement about the Imperial Idea. The scene remains the same, but the time changes: England is now part of the Roman Empire. Rome, standing for the Ideal of Empire, builds the Wall wherever she goes even if not always in masonry. The Wall, symbolic of the Law, divides civilisation, however imperfect, from the barbarous and lawless world that lies outside the Wall. This Wall, we are repeatedly told, is the most wonderful sight in the Empire:

> 'Old men who have followed the Eagles since boyhood say nothing in the Empire is more wonderful than first sight of the Wall! . . . Thirty feet high is the Wall, and on the Picts' side, the North, is a ditch, strewn with blades of old swords and spear-heads set in wood, and tyres of wheels joined by chains.'
>
> (23 171–2)

This massive Wall acts as a barrier between the 'wonderful . . . town behind it' and the dangerous *jungle*[7] outside which is inhabited by the Picts and the Winged Hats, the people without the Law.

The Wall is adorned with a statue of Roma Dea — symbolic of the relationship between the Law and the Imperial Idea. The Wall cannot exist without Rome. Thus in 'A British-Roman Song (A.D. 406)', which appears with the story 'A Centurion of the Thirtieth', the soldiers defending the Wall in Britain invoke the help of Rome:

> *Strong heart with triple armour bound*
> *Beat strongly, for Thy life-blood runs,*
> *Age after Age, the Empire round —*
> *In us Thy Sons,*
>
> *Who, distant from the Seven Hills,*
> *Loving and serving much, require*
> *Thee — Thee to guard 'gainst home-born ills*
> *The Imperial Fire!*
>
> (23 163)

It is worth noting that the Wall is defended not only by Romans but by many different nationalities: ' "Remember, also that the Wall was manned by every breed and race in the Empire. No two towers spoke the same tongue, or worshipped the same Gods." ' (23 174—5) Such internationalism underlines the concept of a universal empire (see Chapter 4). Moreover the significance of Rome seems to reside in the idea that she embodies: although the Roman Empire is shown to be in a state of disorder the Imperial Idea remains imperishable.[8] This is what the rebelling General Maximus learns near the moment of his death. He writes to his captains in Britain: ' " *We have gambled very splendidly against the Gods, but they hold weighted dice, and I must pay the forfeit. Remember, I have been; but Rome is; and Rome will be.*' " ' (23 214)

A second subtheme in the Puck series is that of loyalty and service, two important values of the Law. Hugh in 'The Tree of Justice', even in the presence of the grim King Henry, is not afraid to show his loyalty to Harold the Saxon who is discovered as an old and half-mad wanderer and who dies on Hugh's breast. In the story 'The Wrong Thing' Hal o' the Draft finds satisfaction in his loyalty to his work, so he only laughs when he discovers that the king has knighted him for the carefulness that has saved thirty pounds, not because he is a master craftsman. Parnesius and Pertinax, the captains of the Wall, remain steadfast in the discharge of their duty even though the chances of their success are very slim. 'The Knife and the Naked Chalk' contains the most powerful expression of this theme of loyalty, service and sacrifice. Here the Flint Man sacrifices an eye as the price of iron knives for his people to use against wolves. And worse than that he has to submit to being regarded by his tribe as a god and beyond all human emotions and desires.

Another subtheme is that of conversion — the blending together of different races in the growth of a nation. In 'The Conversion of St Wilfrid' St Wilfrid, Archbishop and missionary, converts the South Saxons, though it is actually his own 'conversion' to which the title of the tale refers. On the islet where he is shipwrecked St Wilfrid learns to value not only the faithfulness of Padda, the tame seal, but also the worth of

Padda's pagan master, Meon. These conversions do lead to the unification of the people and create the bond that is essential for the development of a stable society.

The subject of the growth of a nation is most fully treated in 'Young Men at the Manor'. In the Norman stories the Normans are a conquering and occupying power. Sir Richard Dalyngridge, the Norman Knight, finds himself alone after the battle at Santlache (i.e. the Battle of Hastings). He fights with Hugh the Saxon and spares his life. Then the Saxon saves Richard's life from a group of his own countrymen and takes him to his Manor. Hugh is, however, severely wounded. His sister, the Lady Aelueva, declares that if he dies Richard shall hang, but the imprisoned Richard is rescued next day by De Aquila, the Norman chief, and he gives the Manor to Richard. Ultimately Richard marries the Saxon Lady Aelueva and rules the manor by Saxon custom, while Aquila gives land to her disinherited brother. This is the first step in the blending of conquerors and conquered into one nation. At one stage in the story Hugh says to Richard: ' "Thou hast gone far to conquer England this evening" ', and Richard replies: ' "England must be thine and mine, then. Help me, Hugh, to deal aright with these people." ' And Sir Richard sings aloud:

> *I followed my Duke ere I was a lover,*
> *To take from England fief and fee;*
> *But now this game is the other way over —*
> *But now England hath taken me!*

(23 63)

We have seen that *The Jungle Books* and the Puck books do project a fairly clear picture of the Law. In *The Jungle Books* the Law is presented as a principle of order that is essential for the establishment of an ideal social structure as well as for inner harmony on an individual level. This ideal order is made possible by strict adherence to rules of conduct sanctioned by reason, morality, custom, tradition — the forces of social control which impose upon individuals a code which they break at their peril. The emphasis in *The Jungle Books,* it may be noted, falls heavily upon two basic ingredients of the

Law: moral values and the philosophy of action. The treatment of the Law in the Puck books is not very consistent, one must admit, because here Kipling is primarily concerned with the initiation of children into the history of England as well as the nourishment of their imagination through fiction and romance. His subject however leads him to the topic of the Power of History, which is expressive of various sub-themes of the Law. Of these the most important is the Imperial Idea, which is dealt with especially in *Puck of Pook's Hill,* and which is projected as an essential instrument for promulgating the Law. It is therefore obvious from this study of the four children's books that the Law is a positive force that is crucial for the preservation of civilisation, and that it is composed of interrelated elements — moral values, the Doctrine of Action and the Imperial Idea.

I must admit that for the purpose of this study I may have over-emphasised the didactic element in the children's books. An equally important element of 'education' is the nourishment of the imagination. All of these books educate the youthful imagination in the sense of wonder, variety, distance and depth. Nevertheless the moral element is there. Kipling owns as much when he tells us that he had to contrive that Puck should be read by children first so that it might be read by grown-ups later:

> Yet, since the tales had to be read by children, before people realised that they were meant for grown-ups . . . I worked the material in three or four overlaid tints and textures, which might or might not reveal themselves according to the shifting light of sex, youth, and experience. It was like working lacquer and mother-o'-pearl, a natural combination, into the same scheme as niello and grisaille, and trying not to let the joins show.
>
> (36 182—3)

The Jungle and Puck books are undoubtedly meant to educate. Kipling's whole habit of mind, all of his life, was didactic; he was frankly a preacher and a moralist.

7 Summary and Conclusion

Bless and praise we famous men —
Men of little showing —
For their work continueth,
And their work continueth,
Broad and deep continueth,
Great beyond their knowing!
                                    (*DE* 558)

The complex of ideas which Kipling called the Law had its origin in the circumstances of his early training, in India in particular. The Bombay childhood (1865–71) infused in him what I have termed *sahib*-consciousness — an awareness that one belonged to the ruling class, a belief in authority and a sense of responsibility. The bitter lesson of obedience to authority was driven home during the painful years at Southsea (1871–8). A strong patriotism, enthusiasm for the Empire, discipline and respect for law and order were inculcated in him while he was at United Services College, Westward Ho! (1878–82). The next seven years (1882–9), spent in India as a journalist, were crucial to the development of his ideas: his profession provided him a unique opportunity to understand India, its problems and the way those problems could be solved. An awareness of the threat posed by the Dark Powers and man's compulsive need to defeat these negative forces, profound sense of moral responsibility, devotion to work and faith in the Imperial Idea were the direct results of his experiences in India. In fact it was during the 'Seven Years' Hard' in India that Kipling formed the sympathies and attitudes which later became organised into the general concept of Law that provides the key to much of his work.

Yet Kipling never defines what exactly his Law is. Perhaps a precise definition of such a wide concept is impossible. Moreover it must be remembered that Kipling is not a philosopher; he is primarily an imaginative artist. Therefore one cannot blame him for not giving us a clear-cut statement of his concept of Law. The general outlines of this master-thought, vaguely defined though it may be, are however clear to see if one studies his works as a whole. A careful perusal of his writings reveals that Kipling's Law is composed of three main interrelated elements, namely moral values, the Imperial Idea and the Doctrine of Action. It is with this code of life that Kipling opposes the Dark Powers which he encounters everywhere.

Realisation of a moral order is postulated by Kipling as the first step in the struggle against the Forces of Chaos and Disorder. His vision of a moral order, consisting of such universal values as discipline, devotion to work, positive action, suffering and love, forms the very basis of his philosophy of Law. Various religious and philosophic traditions entered into the shaping of Kipling's moral and ethical views and helped to solidify his conception of Law. In the Judaeo-Christian tradition the Biblical law, the Wesleyan doctrine of vocation and the values of sacrifice, suffering and love influenced him greatly. Similarly, the Islamic emphasis on positive action, law and order seems to have impressed him. Freemasonry confirmed his faith in a universal moral order as well as the brotherhood of mankind. He also admired Mithraism for its emphasis on moral conduct and made it a touchstone for some of his own particular views. His reaction towards Hinduism was negative for it appeared to him that the Hindu attitude towards life was escapist, although he was attracted by the synthesising power of Buddhism, a reformed version of Hinduism. The moral basis of Kipling's Law may therefore be said to be directly related to the moral codes of the diverse religions to which he was exposed.

The Imperial Idea, the second basis of Law, has been the source of much trouble for Kipling's critics and readers. Kipling has too often been condemned for being an imperialist. Put in the context of his times I fail to see how one can expect a sensitive writer to be indifferent to the ideas current at his particular moment in history. While this study of Kipling's philosophy has not denied that he was a conservative and an imperialist, it has forced us to redefine those terms as they apply to his writing. It has been shown above that he was no crude propagandist of British imperialism and that his ideal of empire was based on a philosophic concept of empire as a positive force that imposes a pattern of order on chaos. Kipling's ideal of empire is thus a much larger concept than is generally recognised and it can be traced to the idea of a universal empire based on the principles of law, order, service and sacrifice.

He never questioned the validity of England's civilising mission because he perceived traces of the Imperial Idea in the British Empire. The Empire therefore became another instrument of establishing the Law. Kipling was conscious of the fact that the Empire was not eternal. Just as he believed that the individual matured in virtue under discipline, so did he believe that the colonies would mature. He envisaged something similar to the Commonwealth as the future shape of the Empire: a number of independent nations bound together by a community of purpose and advanced means of communication.

Moreover the Imperial Idea is only a part of Kipling's complex vision; it does not constitute his total view of life. Here it may be observed that the Imperial Idea in itself is not essentially creative though it can be used as a medium for the expression of one's artistic vision.[1] This is precisely what Kipling has suggested. A profound sense of the onslaught of the Dark Powers, of man's helplessness before these negative forces and of his need to defeat these formidable powers creates the essential tension in Kipling's work. The Imperial Idea is a means of articulating this tension. Hence in Kipling's works the Imperial Idea is not only an instrument of establishing the Law on the external level, but it also becomes a sign of the realisation of the self, that is, the establishment of the Law on an inner level.

Disinterested suffering and positive action form the third basic element of Law. Kipling's universe, as indicated by his vision of India, is essentially indifferent or hostile to man. At every turn Kipling sees nameless, shapeless Powers of Darkness which throw him deep into the abyss of nothingness. But these nihilistic tendencies do not lead him to escapism. The universe may be malignant and hostile, yet Kipling believes that man alone is responsible for his own destiny. Either he can let himself be devoured by the Dark Powers or he can, through disinterested suffering and positive action, bring himself out of the limbo of nothingness and thus preserve his individual integrity. Man, according to Kipling, has no reality beyond his own actions: man is what he does, and work is not only a means of ameliorating man's existence in a hostile universe but the very existence itself.

Kipling's world is thus chiefly composed of men of action — administrators, engineers, doctors, soldiers, railwaymen and peasants busy at their jobs. His writings are punctuated by the constant rhythms of daily work. Kipling might have accepted the medieval scholastic's view of matter as that which is to be perfected. The whole purpose of the Law was the gradual perfecting of matter. It was process; it was action. Only by doing could the Law operate. Therefore he praised the men of action and saw man's finest achievement in the way he gave himself to creative work.

The Law can therefore be understood as a principle of order that is essential for the growth of both society and the individual. The nature and function of this master idea of Law is most fully expounded in the fables of *The Jungle Books* in which the Law appears in the form of the code of the Seeonee Wolf Pack. This code consists of rules of conduct that are determined by five basic elements: reason, the common good, ethical values, law-making authority and promulgation, and custom and tradition. In other words the code is sanctioned by the forces of social control which impose upon individuals certain rules which they break at their peril. It is only by strict adherence to this code that an ideal social structure can be evolved.

The Law is however not simply an instrument of the growth of society, but it is also a means of the realisation of the self. Kipling's sense of the importance of society has perhaps been too heavily stressed. His critics and readers have often failed to give due weight to the problem of the individual's isolation and identity with which Kipling is as seriously concerned as with society. The basic question in *Kim,* for example, is: 'Who is Kim — Kim — Kim?' Similarly the Mowgli stories have psychological implications that have not been noted hitherto. These fables can be said to be concerned with the questions of the self and identity: they externalise the inner conflicts that Mowgli undergoes in his struggle for the realisation of the self. The Law is thus an equivalent of order on both social and individual levels. It may be granted that Kipling seems to have given more weight to society because he believes that it is in society alone that the individual can be assured of his integrity. Perhaps Kipling should not have imposed this solution so forcefully; perhaps he should have left it as an unsolved conflict between the individual and society.

Professor Noel Annan, who has written brilliantly on Kipling, has none the less assumed that the Law is only concerned with the well-being of society, not the individual. For Annan the question Kipling asks is 'what holds society . . . together?'[2] And he goes on to relate Kipling with Durkheim in finding the answer to the problem in the forces of social control. Professor Sandison has successfully refuted Annan's position by calling attention to the fact that Kipling is also preoccupied with the problem 'what holds the individual together?'[3] But Sandison goes to the other extreme when he links Kipling with Georges Sorel in the anti-positivist tradition: 'He [Kipling] is not in the least bit interested in society, or its particular morality as absolutes in themselves, but only in so far as they are essential to the self's existence.'[4] Annan had made an exactly opposite statement: 'Kipling is, indeed, seldom interested in the individual as such. He hardly shows how the social process or social morality affects the individual.'[5]

I believe that both Annan and Sandison, while they have given us invaluable insights into the thought of Kipling, have rather flattened and twisted him in order to suit their own particular theories. We do not have to make Kipling into a positivist or an anti-positivist. He was not a thinker or a sociologist; he was primarily an artist. And one cannot expect a logical and consistent philosophy from an imaginative writer. Logical inconsistencies, then, are to be expected, but it must be remembered that emotional attitudes, though frequently at odds with reason, often provide the source of a more rich and complete understanding of life. Kipling, as I have stated above, is concerned with both society and the individual; one cannot separate the one from the other. The Law is a means whereby the individual realises the self and society attains an ideal social order: the two processes are simultaneous and interrelated.

Notes

CHAPTER ONE

1. F. W. L. Adams, *Essays in Modernity: Criticisms and Dialogues* (London, 1899) 185–216.

2. R. W. Buchanan and Sir Walter Besant, *The Voice of 'The Hooligan': A Discussion of Kiplingism* (New York, 1900) 7.

3. For example Lionel Trilling, reviewing it in *The Nation*, 157 (16 Oct 1943) 436, found it was 'verbose in evasion'. Boris Ford, in *Scrutiny*, 11 (1942) 33, felt that 'Eliot should never have lowered himself.' George Orwell writing in *Horizon*, 5 (Feb 1942) 111–25, observed that Eliot defended Kipling 'where he is not defensible'. Anand Mulk Raj, an Indian, reviewing Eliot's article in *Life and Letters Today*, 22 (Mar 1942) 167–70, accused Eliot of neglecting the implications of Kipling's *Weltanschauung*.

4. Bonamy Dobrée, *Rudyard Kipling* (Number 19 in the series 'Writers and their Works', London, 1951) 32.

5. A. R. Sarath Roy, 'Rudyard Kipling Through Hindu Eyes', *North American Review*, 194 (Feb 1914) 274.

6. 'Kipling's Conception of India', *Lippincott's Monthly Magazine*, 94 (Aug 1914) 177.

7. *A Survey of Anglo-Indian Fiction* (London, 1934) 68-74.

8. *The Definitive Edition of Rudyard Kipling's Verse* (London, 1954) 170. Subsequent references to Kipling's verse, unless otherwise indicated, will be to this edition, which will be referred to as *DE*.

9. *The Writings in Prose and Verse of Rudyard Kipling*, 'Outward Bound Edition', 7 (New York, 1897–1937) 10–11. Subsequent references to Kipling's prose works, unless otherwise indicated, will be to this edition.

10. T. S. Eliot, ed., *A Choice of Kipling's Verse* (London, 1941) 30–31.

11. *The Times*, 20 Jan 1936.

CHAPTER TWO

1. André Chevrillon, *Three Studies in English Literature* (New York, 1923) 6–7.

2. Edmund Wilson, 'The Kipling That Nobody Read', *Atlantic Monthly*, 167 (Feb 1941) 201–14; ibid. (Mar 1941) 340–54; reprinted in *The Wound and the Bow* (Boston, 1941) 105–81. Also see Thomas N. Cross, M.D., 'Rudyard Kipling's sense of Identity', *Michigan Quarterly Review*, 4 (Oct 1965) 245–53.

3. For a full treatment of this point see J. M. S. Tompkins, *The Art of Rudyard Kipling* (London, 1959) 119–85.

4. *The United Services College Chronicle*, No. 58, 2 (17 Dec 1894).

5. See H. B. Gray, *Public Schools and the Empire* (London, 1913).

6. *United Services College Chronicle*, Nos. 7–9 (5 Dec 1881, 20 Mar 1882, 3 Jun 1882).

7. The letter is in the Stewart Kipling Collection, Dalhousie University, Halifax.

8. A. P. Cooper, *Rudyard Kipling* (Garden City, 1936) 6.

9. Louis L. Cornell, *Kipling in India* (New York, 1966).

10. Noel Annan, 'Kipling's Place in the History of Ideas', in *Kipling's Mind and Art*, ed. Andrew Rutherford (London, 1964) 102.

11. 'The Council of the Gods', *Pioneer* (18 Feb 1888).

12. This letter is dated 26 Nov 1930. It is part of the Gwynne correspondence in the Stewart Kipling Collection, Halifax, Canada.

13. Dated 25 Jul 1933. Stewart Kipling Collection.

CHAPTER THREE

1. Ecclesiastes 7:29; 2 Kings 8:13; Ecclesiastes 11:1, *The Day's Work;* Matthew 13:57, *Debits and Credits;* Acts 13:1, *Limits and Renewals;* Judges 16:4; Luke 10:38 ff.

2. For information on the Biblical allusions and quotations in Kipling's works, I am indebted to the following sources:

   Anne M. Weygandt, *Kipling's Reading and Its Influence on His Poetry* (Philadelphia, 1939) 159–65.

   Anonymous, 'Kipling and the Bible', *The Kipling Journal*, No. 21 (Mar 1932) 26–7.

   The Rev. Robert B. Gibson, 'The Bible, the Prayer Book and Rudyard Kipling', *The Kipling Journal*, 21 (Apr 1954) 3–6.

3. Weygandt, *Kipling's Reading*, 160, note 10.

4. John Wesley, *The Works of the Rev. John Wesley, A. M.*, 14 vols. (London, 1872) 7 31.

5. Ibid., 123.

6. Ibid., 129.

7. For a full treatment of this subject see W. J. Warner, *The Wesleyan Movement in the Industrial Revolution* (London, 1930).

8. Bonamy Dobrée, *Rudyard Kipling: Realist and Fabulist* (London, 1967) 46.

9. Leading Kipling scholars such as Dr J. M. S. Tompkins, Bonamy Dobrée, Alan Sandison and J. I. M. Stewart are all in agreement on this point.

10. Quoted by Charles Carrington, *Rudyard Kipling: His Life and Work* (London, 1955) 138.

11. Quoted by Carrington, 361.

12. Alan Sandison, *The Wheel of Empire* (New York, 1967) 87.

13. Lockwood Kipling, *Beast and Man in India* (London, 1891) 239.

14. K. B. Rao, *Rudyard Kipling's India* (Oklahoma, 1967) 123—59.

15. Although Kipling states that he was made a Freemason in 1885, it is established by the Minutes of Kipling's Mother Lodge that he was admitted 5 April 1886. The proposition was probably made in the previous year. See Basil M. Bazley, Past Master, Cordwainer Ward Lodge, 'Freemasonry in Kipling's Works', *The Kipling Journal*, 16 (Dec 1949) 13—15 and 17 (Apr 1950) 7—11.

16. Albert Frost, 'R. K.'s Masonic Allusions', *The Kipling Journal*, 13 (Oct 1942) 16—18.

17. Ibid.

CHAPTER FOUR

1. *Cambridge History of the British Empire*, 3 (Cambridge, 1959) 26. Hereafter referred to as *Cambridge History*.

2. Ibid., 27.

3. *Selected Speeches of Lord Beaconsfield*, 2 (London, 1882) 523.

4. Quoted by W. F. Monypenny and G. E. Buckle, *The Life of Benjamin Disraeli*, 4 (London, 1910—20) 335.

5. Quoted by Richard Koebner and Helmut Dan Schmidt, *Imperialism: The Story and Significance of a Political Word, 1840—1960* (Cambridge, 1964) 185.

6. Ibid., 186.

7. Quoted by Richard Faber, *The Vision and the Need: Late Victorian Imperialist Aims* (London, 1966) 62.

8. Ibid., 62.

9. J. A. Froude, *The English in the West Indies* (London, 1888) 182.

10. Thomas Carlyle, *Chartism* (London, 1839) 214.

11. John Ruskin, *Works*, 5 (New York, 1884—91) 29—30.

12. Cited by George Bennett, ed., *The Concept of Empire: Burke to Attlee 1774—1947* (London, 1953) 105.

13. Quoted by Faber, 64.

14. Quoted by Bennett, 104.

15. *Cambridge History*, 3, 159.

16. *Cambridge History*, 5, 541.

17. Sandison, 82.

18. Dobree, *Realist and Fabulist*, 82.

19. Carrington, 275—6.

20. I am indebted to Richard Faber for an insight on this point. See his *The Vision and the Need: Late Victorian Imperialist Aims* (London, 1966).

CHAPTER FIVE

1. In stating that the note of despair is more strongly felt in his later writings, I am conscious of the fact that Kipling does offer the solutions of fellowship, compassion and mirth for the dark states of mind with which he is preoccupied at this stage. Nevertheless the solutions offered do not cancel the poignancy of his deep feelings on the plight of suffering humanity.

2. Morton Cohen, ed., *Rudyard Kipling to Rider Haggard: The Record of a Friendship* (London, 1965) 203.

3. Dobree, *Realist and Fabulist*, 33.

4. George C. Beresford, *Schooldays with Kipling* (London, 1936) 234.

5. It is highly probable that Kipling was exposed to Zoroastrian and other esoteric systems through his connections with the Masonic Lodge at Lahore as well as through A. P. Sinnett, the editor of the *Pioneer*, who was a disciple of Madame Blavatsky. Kipling does not accept the Zoroastrian explanation of the mystery of the universe completely, for he believes in the existence of a greater Power: the signs of the Zodiac, for instance, are only agents of fate to which they themselves, despite their heavenly origin, are subservient.

6. John Milton, *Paradise Lost*, ed. Merritt Y. Hughes (New York, 1962) 223—4.

7. C. S. Lewis, 'Kipling's World', *Literature and Life*, Addresses to the English Association, 1948; reprinted in *The Kipling Journal*, 25 (Sep and Dec 1958) 8—16 and 7—11.

8. *Sunday Times* (6 May 1962) 29.

9. For example see Hilton Brown, *Rudyard Kipling* (London, 1945 54—6, and George Orwell, 'Rudyard Kipling', *Horizon*, 5 (Feb 1942) 111—25.

10. This poem is included in the extremely rare edition of *Rudyard Kipling's Uncollected Verse* (1881—1922) 31—3, printed for private circulation only. A copy of this edition is in the Stewart Kipling Collection, Dalhousie University.

11. Ibid., 32.

12. Ibid., 32—3.

13. Ibid., 33.

14. For an insight into the poem, I am indebted to Dr J. M. S. Tompkins's public lecture on 'If—', which she delivered at Dalhousie University in the winter of 1967.

CHAPTER SIX

1. Ann M. Weygandt, *Kipling's Reading* (Philadelphia, 1939) 85—139.

2. Sir Philip Sidney, *A Defence of Poetry*, ed. J. A. Van Dorsten (Oxford, 1966) 40.

3. Annan, 122.

4. See Kenneth Burke, *The Philosophy of Literary Form: Studies in Symbolic Action* (New York, 1957) 98.

5. G. M. Trevelyan, *A Layman's Love of Letters* (London, 1954) 34—5.

6. For an interpretation of the Puck books, I am greatly indebted to the following source: F. R. Cherry, *The Concept of Law in Rudyard Kipling's Verse* (M.A. thesis, University of Hull, 1958).

7. This jungle should be distinguished from the Indian Jungle of *The Jungle Books*, although potential disorder is symbolised in both.

8. Dr Tompkins has drawn my attention to the fact that the Roman tales are significantly set at the time of the disintegration of the Empire. This may be seen as an analogy of the state of British *raj* in India and elsewhere in the early twentieth century. It has also been pointed out that Hadrian's Wall against the Picts and the Winged Hats resembles the Khyber Pass on the North-West Frontier. However one need not over-emphasize the political analogies in *Puck of Pook's Hill*, though they do exist in some of the stories.

CHAPTER SEVEN

1. Sandison, 195.

2. Annan, 122.

3. Sandison, 105.

4. Ibid., 107.

5. Annan, 123.

Bibliography

This list includes all works cited in this dissertation and some others that I have found helpful but had no opportunity to cite directly.

I PRIMARY SOURCES

(A) Manuscripts and Unpublished Material by Rudyard Kipling

The 'Ballard-Martindell Unauthorized Printings' of the uncollected material from the *Pioneer* and the *Civil and Military Gazette,* Stewart Private Kipling Collection, Halifax.

Material in the Norman Friedman Collection of Kipling, McGill University.

Kipling-Baldwin Correspondence, Stewart Private Kipling Collection, Halifax.

Kipling-Finney Correspondence, Stewart Kipling Collection, Kipling Room, Dalhousie University, Halifax.

Kipling-Gwynne Correspondence, Stewart Private Kipling Collection, Halifax.

Miscellaneous letters, manuscripts and privately printed special editions of Kipling's works, Steward Private Kipling Collection, Halifax and Stewart Kipling Collection, Dalhousie University, Halifax.

Rudyard Kipling's Uncollected Verse: 1881–1922 (Printed for Private Circulation only), Stewart Kipling Collection, Dalhousie University, Halifax.

(B) Works by Rudyard Kipling

Abaft the Funnel. New York, 1909.

Actions and Reactions. New York, 1913.

Barrack-Room Ballads. London 1892.

A Book of Words: Selections from Speeches and Addresses Delivered between 1906—1927. New York, 1928.

A Choice of Kipling's Prose, ed. W. Somerset Maugham. London, 1952.

A Choice of Kipling's Verse, ed. T. S. Eliot. London, 1941.

The Day's Work, 2 vols. New York, 1899.

Departmental Ditties and Ballads and Barrack-Room Ballads. New York, 1899.

Debits and Credits. New York, 1926.

A Diversity of Creatures. New York, 1917.

Early Verse. New York, 1900.

The Eyes of Asia. Garden City, 1918.

The Five Nations. New York, 1913.

From Sea to Sea: Letters of Travel, 1887—1889, 2 vols. New York, 1899.

In Black and White. New York, 1897.

The Irish Guards in the Great War. New York, 1923.

The Jungle Book. New York, 1897.

The Second Jungle Book. New York, 1897.

Just So Stories for Little Children. New York, 1902.

Kim. New York, 1916.

Land and Sea Tales for Boys and Girls. New York, 1937.

Letters of Travel: 1892—1893. New York, 1920.

Life's Handicap. Garden City, 1923.

The Light That Failed. New York, 1899.

Many Inventions. New York, 1899.

Mine Own People. London, 1891.

Naulahka: A Story of West and East. New York, 1897.

The Phantom Rickshaw and Other Stories. Philadelphia, 1898.

Plain Tales from the Hills. New York, 1916.

Rewards and Fairies. New York, 1916.

Rudyard Kipling to Rider Haggard, ed. Morton Cohen. London, 1965.

Rudyard Kipling's Verse, 'Definitive Edition'. London, 1940.

Soldiers Three and Other Military Tales, 2 vols. New York, 1898.

Something of Myself, For My Friends Known and Unknown. Garden City, 1937.

Stalky and Co. New York, 1916.

Traffics and Discoveries. New York, 1916.

Under the Deodars: The Story of the Gadsbys; Wee Willie Winkie. New York, 1916.

War Writings and Poems. New York, 1937.

The Writings in Prose and Verse of Rudyard Kipling, 'Outward Bound Edition', 36 vols. New York, 1897—1937.

The Years Between and Poems From History. New York, 1919.

II SECONDARY SOURCES

(A) Books

Adams, Francis, *Essays in Modernity: Criticisms and Dialogues.* London, 1899.

Archer, William, *Poets of the Younger Generation.* London, 1912.

Arnold, William Delafield, *Oakfield or Fellowship in the East,* 2 vols. London, 1854.

Baker, Joseph E., editor, *The Reinterpretation of Victorian Literature.* Princeton, 1950.

Baldwin, Arthur Windham, *The Macdonald Sisters.* London, 1960.

Ballard, Ellis Ames, *Catalogue Intimate and Descriptive of My Kipling Collection.* Philadelphia: Privately Printed, 1935.

Beerbohm, Max, *The Poets' Corner.* London, 1943.

Bennet, George, editor, *The Concept of Empire; Burke to Attlee: 1774—1947.* London, 1953.

Beresford, George C., *Schooldays with Kipling.* London, 1936.

Bodelsen, C. A., *Studies in Mid-Victorian Imperialism.* Copenhagen, 1960.

———, *Aspects of Kipling's Art.* Manchester, 1964.

Braddy, Nella., *Rudyard Kipling: Son of Empire.* New York, 1942.

Braybrooke, Patrick, *Kipling and His Soldiers.* Philadelphia, 1925.

Brown, Hilton, *Rudyard Kipling.* New York, 1945.

——, editor, *The Sahibs: The Life and Ways of the British in India as Recorded by Themselves.* London, 1948.

Buchan, John, *The Half-Hearted.* London, 1900.

——, *A Lodge in The Wilderness.* London, 1906.

Buchanan, R. W. and Sir Walter Besant, *The Voice of the Hooligan: A Discussion of Kiplingism.* New York, 1900.

Buck, Edward John, *Simla, Past and Present.* 2nd ed.: Bombay, 1925.

Burke, Kenneth, *The Philosophy of Literary Form: Studies in Symbolic Action.* New York, 1957.

Cambridge History of the British Empire, 8 vols. Cambridge, 1929–63.

Carlyle, Thomas, *Works,* 30 vols. New York, 1896.

Carpenter, W. M., *A Few Significant and Important Kipling Items.* Evanston, 1912.

Carrington, Charles, *Rudyard Kipling: His Life and Work.* London, 1955.

Chandler, Lloyd Horwitz, *A Summary of the Works of Rudyard Kipling, Including Items Ascribed to Him.* New York, 1930.

Chesterton, Gilbert Keith, *The Victorian Age in Literature.* London, 1913.

Chevrillon, Andre, *Three Studies in English Literature: Kipling, Galsworthy, Shakespeare,* trans. Florence Simmonds. New York, 1932.

[Clark, William James] G. F. Monkshood (pseudonym), *Rudyard Kipling, the Man and His Work: An Attempt at Appreciation.* London, 1902.

——, *Less Familiar Kipling and Kipliniana.* London, 1936.

Clemens, William, *A Ken of Kipling.* New York, 1899.

Cooper, A. P., *Rudyard Kipling.* Garden City, 1936.

Cornell, Louis L., *Kipling in India.* New York, 1966.

Croft-Cooke, Rupert, *Rudyard Kipling.* London, 1948.

Crooke, William, *The North-Western Provinces of India, Their History and Administration.* London, 1897.

Disraeli, Benjamin, *Selected Speeches of Lord Beaconsfield,* 2 vols. London, 1882.

Dobrée, Bonamy, *The Lamp and the Lute, Studies in Six Modern Authors.* Oxford, 1929.

———, *Rudyard Kipling.* British Council Pamphlet: London, 1951.

———, *Rudyard Kipling: Realist and Fabulist.* London, 1967.

Dodwell, H. H., editor, *The Cambridge History of India: The Indian Empire, 1858–1918,* 6. New York, 1932.

Dunsterville, Lionel Charles, *Stalky's Reminiscences.* London, 1928.

Durand, Ralph, *A Handbook to the Poetry of Rudyard Kipling.* Garden City, 1914.

Elsmie, George Robert, *Thirty-Five Years in the Punjab, 1858–1893.* Edinburgh, 1908.

Elton, Lord, *Imperial Commonwealth.* London, 1945.

Faber, Richard, *The Vision and the Need: Late Victorian Imperialist Aims.* London, 1966.

Falls, Cyril, *Rudyard Kipling: A Critical Study.* New York, 1915.

Fletcher, Angus, *Allegory: The Theory of a Symbolic Mode.* New York, 1964.

Freeman, Edward A., *The History of the Norman Conquest of England,* 6 vols. London, 1867–79.

Froude, J. A., *The English in the West Indies.* London, 1888.

Gardiner, H. G., *Prophets, Priests and Kings.* London, 1914.

Gilbert, Elliot L., *Kipling and the Critics.* New York, 1965.

Gray, H. B., *Public Schools and the Empire.* London, 1913.

Green, Roger Lancelyn, *Kipling and the Children.* London, 1965.

Grolier Club, *Catalogue of the Works of Rudyard Kipling.* New York, 1930.

Harbord, R. E., editor, *A Reader's Guide to the Works of Rudyard Kipling.* Canterbury, 1961–5.

Hart, Walter Morris, *Kipling, the Story Writer.* Berkeley, 1918.

Harte, Bret, *Condensed Novels: New Burlesques.* Second Series:New York, 1902.

Heath-Stubbs, John, *The Darkling Plain.* London, 1950.

Hicks, Granville, *Figures in Transition: A Study of British Literature at the End of the Nineteenth Century.* New York, 1939.

Hobson, John Atkinson, *The War in South Africa: Its Causes and Effects.* London, 1930.

———, *Imperialism: A Study.* London, 1948.

Hopkins, Robert Thurston, *Rudyard Kipling: A Survey of His Literary Art.* London, 1914.

———, *Rudyard Kipling: A Literary Appreciation.* New York, 1915.

———, *Rudyard Kipling: A Character Study, Life, Writings and Literary Landmarks.* London, 1927.

Houghton, Walter E., *The Victorian Frame of Mind, 1830–1870.* New Haven, 1957.

Hunter, Sir William Wilson, *England's Work in India.* London, 1881.

Husain, Syed Sajjad, *Kipling and India.* Dacca, 1965.

Hutton, Maurice, *Many Minds.* Toronto, 1934.

Jackson, Holbrook, *The Eighteen Nineties: A View of Art and Ideas at the Close of the Nineteenth Century.* New York, 1922.

Johnson, Lionel Pigot, *Reviews and Critical Papers.* New York, 1921.

Kernham, Coulson, *Six Famous Living Poets.* London, 1922.

Kincaid, Dennis, *British Social Life in India, 1608–1937.* London, 1938.

Kipling, John Lockwood, *Beast and Man in India: A Popular Sketch of Indian Animals in their Relations with the People.* London, 1891.

The Kipling Journal, issued by The Kipling Society. London, 1927–75.

Knowles, Frederick Lawrence, *A Kipling Primer*. Boston, 1899.

Koebner, Richard and Helmut Dan Schmidt, *Imperialism: The Story and Significance of a Political Word, 1840—1960*. Cambridge, 1964.

Lawton, William Cranston, *Rudyard Kipling, the Artist: A Retrospect and a Prophecy*. New York, 1899.

Le Gallienne, Richard, *Rudyard Kipling: A Criticism*. London, 1900.

Livingston, Flora V., *Bibliography of the Works of Rudyard Kipling*. New York, 1927.

———, *Supplement to Bibliography of the Works of Rudyard Kipling*. Cambridge, Massachusetts, 1938.

Lomer, G. R., *Lest We Forget Rudyard Kipling*. Montreal, 1936.

MacMunn, Sir George Fletcher, *Kipling's Women*. London, 1933.

Mansfield, Milburg, Francisco and A. Wessels, *Kiplingiana*. New York, 1899.

Maraini, Fosco, *Secret Tibet*. New York, 1952.

Martindell, Earnest W., *Bibliography of the Works of Rudyard Kipling, 1881—1923*. London, 1923.

Maurois, André, *Poets and Prophets*. London, 1936.

Mayo, Katherine, *Mother India*. New York, 1927.

Monypenny, W. F. and G. E. Buckle, *Life of Disraeli*, 6 vols. London, 1910—20.

Munson, Arley, *Kipling's India*. Garden City, 1915.

Oaten, Edward Farley, *A Sketch of Anglo-Indian Literature*. London, 1908.

Palmer, John Leslie, *Rudyard Kipling*. London, 1915.

Parker, William B., *The Religion of Mr. Kipling*. New York, 1889.

Peddicord, W. J., *Rudyard Kipling Reviewed: A Review of Rudyard Kipling's 'American Notes'*. Portland, 1900.

Pinto, Vivian De Sola, *Crisis in English Poetry: 1880—1940*. London, 1951.

Ponton, Dorothy, *Rudyard Kipling at home and at work*. Poole, 1953.

Rao, K. Bhaskara, *Rudyard Kipling's India.* Oklahoma, 1967.

Rice, Howard C., *Rudyard Kipling in New England.* Vermont, 1936.

Robertson, William, *The Kipling Guide Book.* Birmingham, 1899.

Routh, H. V., *English Literature and Ideas in the Twentieth Century.* London, 1948.

Ruskin, John, *Works,* 20 vols. New York, 1884—91.

Rutherford, Andrew, editor, *Kipling's Mind and Art.* London, 1964.

Sanderson, Gorham D., *India and British Imperialism.* New York, 1885.

Sandison, Alan, *The Wheel of Empire.* London and New York, 1967.

Scholes, Robert and Robert Kellogg, *The Nature of Narrative.* New York, 1966.

Schrey, Heinz-Horst, Hans Hermann Walz and W. A. Whitehouse, *The Biblical Doctrine of Justice and Law.* London, 1955.

Shanks, Edward, *Rudyard Kipling, A Study in Literature and Political Ideas.* New York, 1940.

Singh, Bhupal, *A Survey of Anglo-Indian Fiction.* London, 1934.

Somervell, David Churchill, *English Thought in the Nineteenth Century.* New York, 1929.

Stewart, James McGregor, *Rudyard Kipling: A Bibliographical Catalogue,* ed. A. W. Yeats. Toronto, 1959.

Stewart, J. I. M., *Eight Modern Writers.* Oxford, 1963.
———, *Rudyard Kipling.* London, 1966.

Thornton, Archibald P., *The Imperial Idea and Its Enemies: A Study in British Power.* London, 1959.

Tompkins, Joyce M. S., *The Art of Rudyard Kipling.* London, 1959.

Trevelyan, George Otto, *The Competition Wallah.* London, 1864.

Trilling, Lionel, *The Liberal Imagination.* Garden City, 1957.

Van De Water, Frederick F., *Kipling's Vermont Feud.* New York, 1937.

Volton, C., *The Allegorical World of Beast in Kipling*. Teramana (Italy), 1937.

Warner, W. J., *The Wesleyan Movement in the Industrial Revolution*. London, 1930.

Wesley, John, *The Works of the Rev. John Wesley, A. M.*, 14 vols. London, 1872.

Wesson, Robert G., *The Imperial Order*. Berkeley and Los Angeles, 1967.

Weygandt, Ann M., *Kipling's Reading and Its Influence on His Poetry*. Philadelphia, 1939.

Wilson, Edmund, *The Wound and the Bow*. Boston, 1941.

Woodruff, Philip, *The Men Who Ruled India*, 2 vols.London, 1953.

Young, W. Arthur, *A Dictionary of the Characters and Scenes in the Stories and Poems of Rudyard Kipling, 1886–1911*. London, 1911.

———, and McGivering, John H., *A Kipling Dictionary*. London and New York, 1967.

(B) Articles

'An Indian Student', 'Kipling's Conception of India' *Lippincott's Monthly Magazine*, 94 (Aug 1914) 177.

Anand, Mulk Raj, 'Mr. Eliot's Kipling', *Life and Letters Today*, 22 (Mar 1942) 167–70.

Annan, Noel, 'Kipling's Place in the History of Ideas', *Victorian Studies*, 3 (Jun 1960) 323–48; reprinted in *Kipling's Mind and Art*, ed. Andrew Rutherford (London, 1964) 97–125.

Anonymous, 'Kipling and the Bible', *Kipling Journal*, No. 21 (Mar 1932) 26–7.

Applin, R. V. K., 'Kipling and Empire Union', *Kipling Journal*, No. 18 (Jun 1931) 43–7.

Auden, Wystan Hugh, 'The Poet of the Encirclement', *New Republic*, 109 (1943) 579–81.

Babbit, Irving, 'Romanticism and the Orient', *Bookman*, 74 (Dec 1931) 352–4.

Bazley, Bazil M., 'Freemasonry in Kipling's Works', *Kipling Journal* (Dec 1949) 13–15 and (Apr 1950) 7–11.

Bushnell, N. S., 'Kipling's Ken of India', *University of Toronto Quarterly,* 27 (Oct 1957) 62—78.

Cazlet, Victor, 'Kipling Versus Internationalism', *Kipling Journal,* No. 40 (Dec 1936) 121—7.

Chaudhuri, Nirad C., 'The Finest Story About India — in English', *Encounter,* 7 (Apr 1957) 47—53.

Collins, J. P., 'Rudyard Kipling at Lahore', *The Nineteenth Century and After,* 121 (Jan 1937) 80—90.

Dobree, Bonamy, 'Kipling the Visionary', *Kipling Journal,* 23 (Apr 1956) 3—5.

Edwards, Michael, 'Rudyard Kipling and the Imperial Imagination', *Twentieth Century,* 153 (Jun 1953) 443—54.

Eliot, T. S., 'Introduction', *A Choice of Kipling's Verse* (London, 1941).

———, 'Rudyard Kipling', *Mercure de France,* 325 (Jan 1959) 5—15; translated as 'The Unfading Genius of Rudyard Kipling', *Kipling Journal,* 26, No. 129 (Mar 1959) 9—12.

Faber, Marjorie, 'The Apostle of an Empire', *New York Times Book Review* (26 Sep 1943) 1, 22.

Fleming, Alice Macdonald [Kipling], 'Some Reminiscences of My Brother', *Kipling Journal,* No. 44 (Dec 1937) 116—21.

———, 'Some Childhood Memories of Rudyard Kipling', *Chambers's Journal,* Series 8 (Mar 1939) 169.

Ford, Boris, 'A Case For Kipling', *Scrutiny,* 9 (1942—3) 23—33.

Frost, Albert, 'Rudyard Kipling's Masonic Allusions', *Kipling Journal,* No. 25 (Oct 1942) 16—18.

Gerber, Helmut E. and Edward Lautherbach, editors, 'Rudyard Kipling: An Annotated Bibliography of Writings About Him', *English Fiction in Transition,* 3 (1960) Nos. 3—5.

Gibbon, Robert B., 'The Bible, the Prayer Book and Rudyard Kipling', *Kipling Journal,* 21 (Apr 1954) 3—6.

Harris, Ray Baker, 'Freemasonry', *Encyclopaedia Britannica,* 24 vols. 9 (Chicago, 1966) 840—4.

Jack, P. M., 'Kipling, the Poet of Imperialism', *New York Times Book Review* (27 Oct 1940) 5.

Johnston, Ronald Carlyle, 'Fable', *Encyclopaedia Britannica*, 24 vols. 9 (Chicago, 1967) 22–4.

Lewis, Clive Staples, 'Kipling's World', *Literature and Life*, Addresses to the English Association, 1948; reprinted in *They Asked For a Paper* (London, 1962) 72–92.

McLuhan, H. M., 'Kipling and Forster', *Sewanee Review*, 52 (1944) 332–43.

McMunn, Sir George Fletcher, 'Some Kipling Origins', *Blackwood's Magazine*, 222 (Aug 1927) 145–54.

Montgomery, M., 'The Nationality of Kipling's Kim', *Germanische-Romanische Monatschrift*, (Oct–Nov 1914) 587–8.

Mullin, E. H., 'Stevenson, Kipling and Anglo-Saxon Imperialism', *Book Buyer*, 18 (1899) 85–90.

Norton, Charles Eliot, 'The Poetry of Rudyard Kipling', *Atlantic Monthly*, 79 (Jan 1897) 111–15.

Orwell, George, 'Rudyard Kipling', *Horizon*, 5 (Feb 1942) 111–25; reprinted in *Critical Essays* (London, 1946) 100–13.

Packard, Winthrop, 'Rudyard Kipling: An Estimate', *National Magazine*, 10 (Apr 1899) 77–9.

Powever, William R., 'Uncollected Kipling Items', *Notes and Queries*, 12th Series, 7 (Aug 1920) 136.

Robinson, Edward Kay, 'Kipling in India: Reminiscences by the Editor of the Newspaper on Which Kipling Served at Lahore', *McClure's Magazine*, 7 (Jul 1896) 99–109.

———, 'Mr. Kipling as a Journalist', *Academy*, 4 (London, Mar 1899) 284–6.

Roy, Sarath A. R., 'Rudyard Kipling Seen Through Hindu Eyes', *North American Review*, 199 (Feb 1914) 271–81.

Scott-Giles, C. W., 'Historical Background of some "Puck" Stories', *Kipling Journal*, 28 (Jun 1961) 15–16.

Stevenson, Lionel, 'The Ideas in Kipling's Poetry', *University of Toronto Quarterly*, 1 (Jul 1932) 467–89.

———, 'The Later Victorian Poets: Rudyard Kipling', *The Victorian Poets: A Guide to Research*, ed. Frederic E. Faverty (Cambridge, Massachusetts, 1956) 261–2.

Thompson, C. Patrick, 'The White-faced Boy of Lahore', *World Review*, 8 (Feb 1929) 56—7.

Trilling, Lionel, 'Mr. Eliot's Kipling', *The Nation*, 157 (1943) 436, 440—2; reprinted in *Kipling's Mind and Art*, ed. Andrew Rutherford (London, 1964) 85—96.

Varley, Henry Leland, 'Imperialism and Rudyard Kipling', *Journal of the History of Ideas*, 14 (Jan 1953) 124—35.

Ward, Harry Frederick, 'The Religion of Kipling', *Methodist Review*, 82 (1900) 262—9.

Waterhouse, Francis Ashbury, 'The Literary Fortunes of Kipling', *Yale Review*, 10 (Jul 1912) 817—31.

West, Rebecca, 'Rudyard Kipling', *New Statesman and Nation*, 11 (Jan 1936) 112—14.

Wilson, Edmund, 'The Kipling That Nobody Read', *Atlantic Monthly*, 167 (Feb 1941) 201—14 and (Mar 1941) 340—54; reprinted in *The Wound and the Bow* (Boston, 1941) 105—81.

Yeats, A. W., 'The Genesis of "The Recessional" ', *University of Texas Studies in English*, 31 (1952) 97—108.

———, 'Kipling, Twenty Years After', *Dalhousie Review*, 36 (1956) 59—64.

(C) *Unpublished Material*

Baxter, B. W. J., *The Poetry in Kipling's Verse*. Master's thesis. Leeds University, 1956.

Brown, E. I., *Burma and Kipling*. Master's thesis. University of Southern California, 1926.

Buckland, Roscoe L., *Anglo-Saxonism in America, 1880-1898*. Ph.D. thesis. State University of Iowa, 1955.

Campbell, Bertha Belle, *Kipling's Women*. Master's thesis. State University of Iowa, 1919.

Cherry, F. R., *The Concept of the Law in Rudyard Kipling's Verse*. Master's thesis. University of Hull, 1958.

Derrett, M. E., *The Novel about India since Independence, written by Indians in English*. Master's thesis. London University, 1964.

Gilbert, Elliot L., *A Case For Kipling.* Ph.D. thesis. Cornell University, 1963.

Giles, James Richard, *A Study of the Concept of Atvaism in the Writings of Rudyard Kipling, Frank Norris, and Jack London.* Ph.D. thesis. University of Texas, 1966.

Husain, S. S., *Rudyard Kipling and India.* Ph.D. thesis. Nottingham University, 1952.

Ray, Bessie L., *Kipling's Pictures of the Relation of the Two Races in India.* Master's thesis. Columbia University, 1931.

Rouse, J. J., *The Literary Reputation of Rudyard Kipling: A Study of the criticism of Kipling's works in British periodicals from 1886–1960.* Ph.D. thesis. New York University, 1963.

Singh, Kranti, *Kipling's India.* Ph.D. thesis. London University, 1966.

Stanton, Millet, *Rudyard Kipling: A Study of His Thought and Social Criticism.* Ph.D. thesis. Indiana University, 1958.

Varley, Henry L., *A Study in the career of Rudyard Kipling.* Ph.D. thesis. Wisconsin University, 1954.

Yeats, A. W., *Kipling Collections in the James McGregor Stewart and the University of Texas Libraries: An Appraisal of Resources for Literary Investigation.* Ph.D. thesis. University of Texas, 1962.

Index

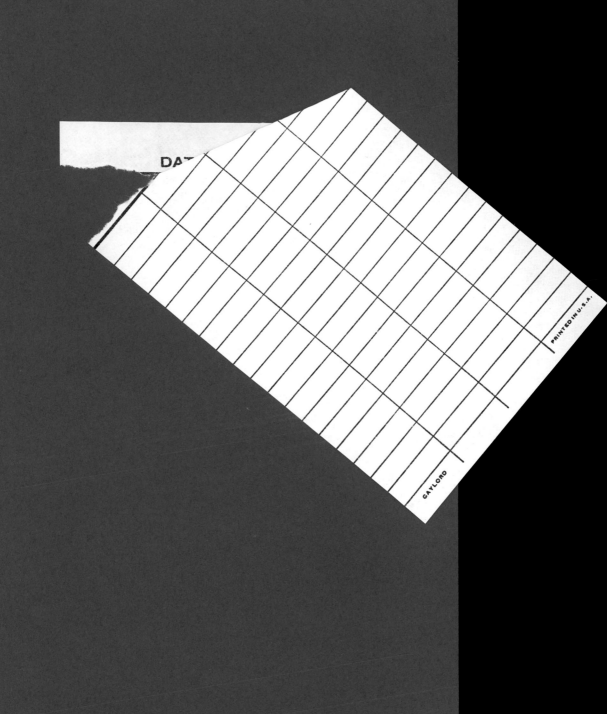

DAT

GAYLORD   PRINTED IN U.S.A.